When the
Forgotten
Borough Reigned

The 1964
Little League
World Champions

Jeff Ingber

WHEN THE FORGOTTEN BOROUGH REIGNED: THE 1964 LITTLE LEAGUE WORLD SERIES

For information about this title or to order other books and/or electronic media, contact Jeff Ingber at jingber@gmail.com or www.jeffingber.com.

ISBN: 978-0-9854100-6-3 (softcover)
        978-1-7371713-0-0 (hardcover)
        978-0-9854100-9-4 (eBook)

Cover design by Arielle Morris

For Kayla, Maddie, and Sienna, who bring such joy

11 | 18 | 23

To PETE,

I HOPE YOU ENJOY!

YOUR PAL,

JEFF

*For those of you who don't know, Staten Island
is like Brooklyn and New Jersey had a baby.*
—"Staten Island Summer" (2015 film)

CONTENTS

PREFACE

FEW IMAGES ARE AS evocative of America as boys in uniforms playing baseball on a natural grass field with a dirt diamond. Little League baseball, the world's largest organized youth sports program, is a rite enjoyed annually by millions throughout every U.S. state and in more than eighty countries. Each August, the culmination of play is its well-known "World Series" held in picturesque Williamsport, Pennsylvania.

The Little League World Series is, statistically, the hardest tournament globally to win. Each one is special. The 1964 tournament, held on the 25th anniversary of the founding of Little League baseball, was uniquely so. The final Series game was won on a no-hitter spun by a pitcher on an All-Star team from the middle of Staten Island, the "forgotten borough," which had more in common with the American heartland than the rest of New York City. Not only had a Big Apple team never before even qualified for the World Series, but it was the first time a U.S. team defeated an international one—in that case, the Obispado All-Stars from Monterrey, Mexico—for the championship. The members of the victorious Mid-Island Little League team were treated to a ticker-tape parade in lower Manhattan (the only kids ever to be so honored) and a reception by the mayor as well as meetings with celebrities such as Lucille Ball and baseball icons, including Casey Stengel. A gaggle of prominent politicians clamored for photo ops with the country's newest darlings.

In 1964, a transformational year that has been characterized as the last one of "American innocence," baseball firmly held its position as the treasured national pastime. The reverence for the sport was particularly strong in Staten Island, which remained a bastion of pastoral living and traditional values sheltered from the dramatic societal and cultural makeover that much of the nation was undergoing.

In November of that year, the Verrazzano-Narrows Bridge opened, linking Staten Island with Brooklyn. A tidal wave of transformation quickly swept through the Island. But, months before then, there was a magical summer during which fourteen boys, none older than twelve, experienced a degree of fame few adults ever do while uniting the borough and city in frenzied celebration.

CHAPTER 1
Isolation

*We were country boys in the forgotten borough, and that's
exactly how we wanted it to be.*

—Jeff Paul

THE TRIANGULAR Staten Island is separated from New
Jersey by the Kill Van Kull, a tidal strait three miles long
and only a fifth of a mile wide, and from the rest of New
York City by New York Bay. The first European to sight the
island was Giovanni da Verrazzano, a Florentine explorer
in the service of King Francois I of France who had been
commissioned to find a new trade route to Asia. In April
1524, Verrazzano sailed through The Narrows, the waterway
connecting Upper and Lower New York Bays, and anchored
for one night.

Henry Hudson, sailing for the Dutch East India
Company and also seeking a westerly passage to Asia,
arrived in September 1609. He named the landmass "Staaten
Eylandt" ("States Island") to honor the States General,

Holland's bicameral legislature, and paved the way for the Dutch to colonize it.[1]

Staten Island played a prominent role during the Revolutionary War due to its strategic location at the mouth of New York Harbor, the prime gateway into the city.[2] In November 1783, the final shot of that war—signaling, in a sense, the beginning of the new nation—was fired from a cannon on a departing frigate at the military installation on the Staten Island side of the Narrows (later named "Fort Wadsworth"), where crowds stood jeering the redcoats.

After many decades of debate, Staten Island, although closer to New Jersey, formally became a part of New York in 1833 when the two states agreed that New York would obtain the rights to the Island and the Lower New York Bay south to Raritan Bay while New Jersey would hold the rights over the water on the west side of the Island down to Sandy Hook Bay. During the opening half of the 19th century, the Island and its economy was centered around scattered farms as well as tiny shore fishing villages where oysters were the prized bounty. Among many others, Henry David Thoreau, who spent part of 1843 on Staten Island (before he famously went to live in a cabin in the woods by Walden Pond), was struck by the natural beauty around him. "This is in all respects a very pleasant residence. Much more rural than you would expect in the vicinity of New York."

The well-to-do were drawn to this pristine locale, where they built lavish homes, grand hotels, yacht and country clubs, and hunting preserves.[3] After the Civil War, Midland

and South Beaches were developed on the east shore and became popular resorts, offering bathing facilities, an amusement park, and vacation bungalows.

In 1894, spurred by the poor quality of public services such as roads and sewage systems, schools, and police and fire squads, a non-binding referendum was held regarding joining with the four boroughs. Staten Islanders overwhelmingly supported consolidation, which was formally accomplished four years later. At the time, most of the Island's 60 square miles, particularly those in the central, southern, and western areas, remained undeveloped and rife with woodlands, lakes, streams, and swamps. While the other boroughs continued to industrialize and incur rapid population growth, Staten Island, only five miles from Manhattan and three miles from Brooklyn by water, stayed rural.

The Island's seclusion eased when, between 1928 and 1931, three bridges were built by the Port Authority of New York providing links to New Jersey. But it stayed unconnected with the City subway system and the other boroughs other than via various ferries.[4] Most of those ferry systems are long gone, with the exception of the Staten Island Ferry, two centuries old, which continues to ply the waters of New York Harbor, affording stunning views of the Statue of Liberty, Ellis Island, and the Manhattan skyline during a free 25-minute ride.[5] The Ferry has been a companion over the years to parades of ships bearing immigrants to the New World.

In 1964, most of Staten Island's neighborhoods remained bucolic, with each exhibiting its own characters and idiosyncrasies. Men supplemented their income by hunting and trapping, or crabbing on the seashore. Winter turned the ubiquitous ponds into ice-skating opportunities. Stores of the mom-and-pop variety sold staples from local farms, along with kids' favorites, including penny candy, bubble gum cigars, and jawbreakers. Cars were highly desired, as residents complained that waiting for a trolley or bus "took forever." Often, multiple connections were needed to arrive at a destination.

Jay Price, who grew up in Staten Island and was a longtime sportswriter for the *Staten Island Advance*, recalled, "You could drive south down Hylan Boulevard, a major commercial road that runs the length of the east side of the Island, and, once you got past New Dorp, you'd go seven miles without a light or stop sign. It was country there—horse trails, truck farms, and the like." In Tottenville on the South Shore, Father Drumgoole's Mission of the Immaculate Virgin at Mount Loretto, a 600-acre property dedicated to the care of orphaned children, operated the largest dairy farm in the state and the third largest in the country, producing up to a thousand quarts of milk daily.

Staten Island's remoteness and sparse population led it to possess limited political clout, allowing New York State officials to engage in a pattern of situating entities there deemed undesirable. They included institutions for the mentally challenged, prisons, homeless shelters, and a tuberculosis sanatorium, as well as the Fresh Kills Landfill, which opened in 1948 as a "temporary" solution to New York City's trash-disposal problem. Due to rampant municipal corruption, it continued to mushroom until it became the world's largest dump. more than 3,000 fetid acres and five hundred feet high in certain spots, attracting the ever-present seagulls and feral dogs, it operated for more than 50 years.

Every member of the 1964 Mid-Island Little League (MILL) team, when reflecting back almost six decades on his childhood, waxed nostalgic. Common summer memories included dashing out of the house after breakfast, playing sports all day, racing home for dinner, and again gathering with other kids in the evening for games such as hide-and-go-seek, kick-the-can, red rover, and jacks before returning home when the streetlights came on. Moms and dads would sit on their front porch and watch out for neighbors' kids as their own. Boys would ride bikes throughout central Staten Island, with baseball cards affixed to the spokes as flaps. As they meandered, they'd find hay fields to romp around in and vacant lots with a basketball hoop or small diamond and a pickup game going on.

Other recurrent recollections among those who grew up in Staten Island in the '50s and early '60s was that every neighborhood boasted its own movie theater, ice cream shoppe, pizza parlor, and corner bar. And ballfields that were prized and heavily used. Each one was a building block of the miracle that emerged in the summer of 1964.

A sports marvel that temporarily overshadowed the growing significance, for better and for worse, of what would be the greatest gamechanger in the history of Staten Island—"The Bridge."

CHAPTER 2
The Bridge

At the end of Quinlan Avenue, the road turned to dirt and entered woods where you could explore nature to your heart's content. But by the time I turned thirteen, those woods had been ripped up and paved over.

—Billy Ebner

TO THIS DAY, there are said to be two types of people on Staten Island: those whose families arrived before the Verrazzano-Narrows Bridge opened and those whose families came later.

The earliest concept for a crossing between Brooklyn and Staten Island over the Narrows was a rail tunnel proposed in 1888 by the Baltimore and Ohio Railroad, which would have expanded the route of its Staten Island North Shore line. Construction commenced, but after 150 feet had been dug on each side, financial constraints and delays in the approval process killed the project. In 1921, the New York State Legislature authorized the building of a twin-tube Brooklyn-Staten Island subway-and-automobile tunnel. Partial excavation of the access shafts at each end of the Narrows began before the work was stopped due to unexpected costs.[6] The focus on a tunnel link remained until the Golden Gate Bridge opened in 1937. The construction of that bridge provided builders with vital experience in erecting a lengthy suspension span.

In 1946, Robert Moses, the famed New York power broker whose works, which define the New York City area, include numerous parks, highways, housing projects, and notable complexes such as Lincoln Center and Jones Beach State Park, had been chairing the Triborough Bridge and Tunnel Authority for more than a decade.[7] Moses, who abhorred tunnels for their lack of aesthetics, proposed constructing the world's longest bridge across the Narrows, with the two Army forts that guarded New York Harbor— Fort Hamilton in Brooklyn and Fort Wadsworth in Staten Island—as end points. Moses argued that among the valuable purposes the bridge would serve would be to spur industrial growth on Staten Island and circumnavigate traffic away from Manhattan while connecting the interstate highway system along the East Coast.

Moses pushed to create additional access to the new bridge by extending Brooklyn's Gowanus Expressway by way of Seventh Avenue, cutting through the middle of Bay Ridge, a largely white, Catholic neighborhood located in the southwest corner of the borough. That plan, which required demolition of hundreds of homes and the displacement of thousands of residents via eminent domain, drew vehement but unsuccessful opposition from the community. The Staten Island response to the bridge was mixed. Access to points east would be far easier. In a sense, the modern day Moses would lead them out of their geographic bondage. And many residents welcomed the economic benefits that a firmer connection to the rest of the city would provide as well as the cachet of having one of the world's celebrated bridges in their backyard. Others were outspoken about the threat to the Island's rustic character from outsiders expected to swarm there seeking an "American Dream" suburban lifestyle. The dissenters' protests were reinforced when, even before the formal announcement of the approval of the bridge, land developers and speculators rushed in, triggering a rise in real estate values.

Moses hired Othmar Amman, his collaborator in building the Bronx-Whitestone, Throgs Neck, and Triborough bridges, to design the Verrazzano. Amman, who believed that aesthetics and functionality deserve equal prominence, characterized his concept for the bridge as "an enormous object drawn as faintly as possible" and, thus, determined to paint it gray.

Ground for the Verrazzano-Narrows Bridge was broken in August 1959 at Fort Wadsworth. Gradually, the elegant, rainbow-shaped structure rose above the Narrows. Two-and-a-half-miles long in total and supported by four cables hung from towers close to 700 feet high, it would require more than five years to complete. The crossing was a creation so vast that the curvature of the earth needed to be taken into account as a component of its design.

"To us simple folk on Staten Island," recalled Eddie Godnig, MILL's right fielder, "the Verrazzano was one of the world's man-made wonders, like the Great Pyramid. My dad, a design engineer, was fascinated by its construction. He would drive me over to our side of the bridge as it was being built and explain to me facets of its construction and how amazing it was."

By the summer of 1964, also nearing completion was the six-lane Staten Island Expressway, built to provide access to the Verrazzano, which in the short term would have a more significant impact on Mid-Island than the bridge itself. The Expressway surfaced down the block from the Meiers Corners house of Billy Ebner, MILL's first baseman. "My neighborhood then was like an extended, close-knit family," Ebner recounted. "Everyone—policemen, firemen, teachers, and bank tellers—seemed to know each other. Almost all the houses were different, which gave it character." One day, Ebner awoke to the sound of earth movers. "All of a sudden, huge machinery were near our doorstep every day, literally opening up the wilderness. They took down hundreds of trees just in my immediate area."

One day, Joe Nugent, older brother of Bobby Nugent, MILL's third baseman and third pitcher, stood on the sidewalk watching in awe as a house was carried away on a tractor trailer from Clermont Place, a street split in half by the new expressway, south to a large hole on Mountainview

Avenue.[8] "Growing up on Staten Island in the '50s and early '60s," Nugent reminisced, "was perfection. I wouldn't change a thing about that place or time. Then the bridge and the expressway came. After that, nothing was the same."

Nearly 12,000 men would work on the bridge's construction, with up to a thousand on the site in a single day. Most were "Skywalkers," members of local ironworkers unions who performed the demanding work of lifting and welding steel, driving rivets, spinning cable, pouring concrete, and the like.[9] And they did so in extremely dangerous and difficult conditions, having to walk across steel girders averaging two-feet wide but as narrow as six inches, often in a strong wind and at times in the rain or cold.

One of the Skywalkers was Lawrence Paul, a full-blooded Native American born and raised on the Saint Regis Mohawk Reservation in Hogansburg, New York, near the St. Lawrence River and the Canadian border. With job opportunities limited, after graduating high school, Paul joined the Air Force. While stationed at the Offutt Air Base outside of Omaha, Nebraska, he met his future wife, LaVonne. After the end of his military service, Paul followed longstanding Mohawk tradition and became an ironworker.

In 1957, the Pauls moved to Brooklyn's Dean Street in a Crown Heights section that had morphed into a Native-American enclave. It was an era when innumerable Brooklyn families chose to relocate to Staten Island for its tranquility, open spaces, and relatively cheap housing. The Pauls soon followed suit, purchasing a home a stone's throw from Billy Ebner's. With LaVonne as a stay-at-home mom, the Pauls raised two girls and a boy, Jeff, who would become a vital cog in the engine that was the MILL All-Star team of 1964.

CHAPTER 3
1964

*As a twelve-year-old, I was blissfully unaware of all going on
in the world then. I ate, breathed, and dreamt baseball.*

—Danny Yaccarino

THE UNITED STATES entered the 1960s with rising
prosperity and quality of life, a tranquil civil society, and
peace in hand. Planning was underway for an extravaganza
designed to display America's ideal future—the New York
City World's Fair—which opened in April 1964 in Flushing
Meadows in the borough of Queens. (Robert Moses was
President of the World's Fair and its driving force.) The
Fair, which drew over 51 million visitors during its two six-
month seasons, featured more than 140 pavilions and 110
restaurants, with 80 nations, 24 states, and more than 45
corporations sponsoring exhibits or attractions. With a
theme of "Peace Through Understanding," the Fair focused
on the promise that science, technology, and a free capi-
talist society were the keys to building a better tomorrow.

The 1960s were years of transformational change, affecting societal, political, scientific, military, and economic arenas—indeed, America's very identity. During that decade, the country landed men on the moon, came close to nuclear confrontation with the former Soviet Union, grieved for three slain national figures, saw its new heavyweight champion join the Nation of Islam, and was "invaded" by the Beatles, who symbolized the divide between generations. In the mid to late '60s, capped by the 1969 Woodstock Music Festival, the country went "counterculture" against all sorts of commonly accepted norms.

1964, when the baby boomer generation capped off, was a seminal time in the fight against pervasive racial discrimination. The most influential civil rights figure of the day, Dr. Martin Luther King, had during the previous August led a massive March on Washington in which he delivered his stirring "I Have a Dream" address.[10] Spurred by King's leadership, in 1964, the civil rights movement achieved a number of successes. Notably, in January, ratification was completed of the 24th Amendment of the Constitution, which prohibited both Congress and the states from conditioning the right to vote in federal elections on payment of a poll tax, which disproportionately affected African-American voters.

In May 1964, President Lyndon Johnson, who had succeeded the slain John F. Kennedy and who would be elected in November to a full term as President in a landslide over Barry Goldwater, declared that he would transform the United States into a "Great Society" in which poverty, lack of quality education and medical care, and racial inequality all were eradicated. On July 2, during "Freedom Summer," Johnson signed into law the momentous Civil Rights Act of 1964, banning discrimination in public places, providing for the integration of schools and other public facilities, and making it illegal for employers to discriminate based on race, color, religion, sex, or national origin.[11] Later that month, the first of a series of devastating race-related riots that would rip through American cities began in Harlem following the shooting of fifteen-year-old James Powell by a white off-duty police officer. The eruption of violence soon spread to Brooklyn's Bedford-Stuyvesant neighborhood and continued for six days.

Other rights crusades were stirring, including a second wave of the feminist movement (the first was the decades-long effort to gain women's suffrage) triggered in 1963 by the book *The Feminine Mystique,* written by Betty Friedan, which decried the notion that women were naturally fulfilled by devoting their lives to being housewives and mothers. During 1964, *The Feminine Mystique* became the bestselling nonfiction book, with more than one million copies sold.[12] Also that year, the first public demonstration for gay rights in U.S. history occurred outside the Army Building in lower Manhattan when gay and straight men and women joined to protest the military's discriminatory policies. Taking place on a September Saturday, it was little seen and received no media attention.[13] Unlike other movements, the one for gay rights would have to wait several more years before gaining traction.

Starting in the summer of 1964, tensions in the Far East escalated into the Vietnam War, leading to massive anti-war marches and other protests in the U.S. Certain activists grew radical, embracing domestic terrorism. In millions of households, the patriotism and anti-communist bent of fathers and mothers who had served in the armed forces or otherwise supported the World War II and Korean War efforts were challenged by rebellious children who countered their perceived desire for material wealth with an emphasis on self-fulfillment.

In 1964, Staten Island, with 225,000 residents mostly living in one-family houses, stood apart from the rest of the City in a number of respects. One was ethnic composition. The Island was "whiter" and more homogenous, with relatively few African-, Asian-, or Hispanic-Americans. (There were historic African-American communities scattered about in Mid-Island and elsewhere, and the MILL team members noted that there was no racial bias or tension in the neighborhoods of their youth.) As with the rest of the nation, Staten Island ultimately would be profoundly influenced by the civil rights developments that took place that year.

Baseball, a bastion of ageless tradition, was not unaffected by national events. In fact, it was undergoing its own cultural transformation as the number of African-American and Latino major-league players increased. Yet baseball's rituals, and its principles of sportsmanship, competition, and fair play within a pre-defined set of rules, remained firm.

Chapter 3

By 1964, in its 25th year, Little League baseball had become a distinct component of the nation's civil fabric.[14] Even more than its professional counterpart, Little League represented, to paraphrase the words of the Terence Mann character in *Field of Dreams*, all that is good in America. How did this beloved American institution arise? And what led it to grab hold of the hearts and minds of youth across the nation and beyond?

CHAPTER 4
Origins

Once you've lived in the land of baseball, you're a permanent resident.

—Bobby Nugent

THE VISION OF WHAT came to be Little League baseball was imagined in 1938 by 28-year-old Carl Stotz, chief clerk for the Pure Oil Company. A son of German-Americans, Stotz had lived his entire life in Williamsport, a central Pennsylvania town with a rich minor league history. While Stotz was playing catch with his two nephews, he asked them, "How would you like to be on a regular team, with uniforms, a new ball for every game, and bats you can really swing?" Years later, Stotz would reflect on that moment. "Somewhere deep inside, beyond my consciousness, the love of baseball lay waiting for an opportunity to get out."

Stotz decided to organize a neighborhood-based, volunteer-operated baseball program as a summer activity for pre-teen boys, not merely for the joy of the game but, additionally, to counter social isolation and juvenile delinquency.[15] He envisioned a miniaturized version of big-league baseball with players competing on manicured fields before umpires calling balls and strikes and score-keepers tracking statistics. Fundamental to Stotz's concept was his insistence on capturing the sounds, sights, smells, and crowds—the entirety of what renders baseball special.

In 1939, with the help of his wife Grayce, friends Bert and George Bebble, and others, Stotz canvassed local businesses. After dozens of rejections, he convinced three (Lycoming Dairy, Lundy Lumber, and Jumbo Pretzel) to be sponsors. The three-team association became known as the "Little League."

Stotz experimented to determine how best to set the dimensions of the playing field so as to balance the advantages for the offense and defense. He concluded that the ideal Little League field was roughly two-thirds the size of a professional one. Thus, he spaced the bases 60 feet apart, placed the pitcher's mound 38 feet from home plate (later lengthened to 44 feet and then 46 feet), and set the outfield fence at 200 feet from home plate. Stotz introduced lighter, shorter bats and gloves geared to children's bodies.

Rules covering games were designed to parallel those of conventional baseball, but with a number of accommodations to the physical and emotional immaturity of the players. For example, runners were not allowed to leave their base until the ball had been delivered by the pitcher and passed the plate. Stotz also limited the length of Little League games to six innings, plus extra innings as needed.

Stotz and his supporters set up a crude ballfield on a vacant lot, grading the surface, marking out a baseball diamond with bases constructed from duck cloth, building a backstop behind a home plate carved out of rubber, and planting grass. Its location was fitting—across the street from the outfield fence of Bowman Field (now BB&T Ballpark, home of the Class A Williamsport Crosscutters, a Philadelphia Phillies affiliate), an historic minor league ballpark that's the oldest in Pennsylvania and second oldest in the nation.

The first Little League game was held on a Tuesday afternoon in June 1939, with Lundy Lumber trouncing Lycoming Dairy, the team managed by Stotz, 23–8. By 1942, a new field (known as "Original Field") was built into the side of a hill located in the city's Max M. Brown Memorial Park, which allowed for far more spectators. A year later, a home run fence was added (until that time, all homers were inside-the-park). Two years later, the world's first electronic scoreboard was built for Original Field.

Critical to the Little League's success was the organizational structure that developed based around the concept of leagues, each identified with the participating community and composed of four to eight teams. To be eligible for Little League play, a boy must not have reached his 13th birthday before August 1 of the current year. To ensure that Little League remained a community-based program, participants in a local league are required to live or attend school within set physical boundaries. Typically, from twelve to fifteen players are selected for each team via tryouts. Boys not selected are accommodated in a "farm" or "minor" league.[16]

Following World War II, the Little League expanded rapidly, mirroring the attitudes and aspirations of American parents and their growing number of children. This was particularly true for suburban and rural locales, where amateur sports offered the opportunity for kids and their parents to readily socialize.

In 1947, Little League grew beyond Pennsylvania to western New Jersey. That year saw the inauguration of "World Series" competition (branded initially as the "Little League National Tournament"), but involving several teams rather than a series of games between just the two finalists. In the championship game, 2,500 fans thronged Original Field to watch the Maynard Midgets of Williamsport defeat a team from Lock Haven, Pennsylvania, Williamsport's upriver neighbor. The results were printed in newspapers nationally, and the ensuing publicity helped spread the formation of leagues.

The following year, the Little League obtained its first corporate sponsor, U.S. Rubber (now Uniroyal), which assumed a crucial role in the evolution of Little League baseball, providing operating expertise and large financial grants.[17] That year, Lock Haven returned to the World Series and defeated a team from St. Petersburg, Florida, in the final game, with highlights captured in newsreels (at the time a regular feature at movie theaters) seen by tens of millions.

In 1949, Little League's cachet soared when it was featured in two popular national magazines—the *Saturday*

Evening Post and *Life*. A play-by-play account of the final game of that year's World Series, won by a team from Hammonton, New Jersey, was broadcast over a hundred NBC radio stations. Stotz received requests from across the country for information on forming local leagues. In 1950, the first ones outside the U.S. were established at each end of the Panama Canal at military bases. Canada soon followed suit, as did Cuba after Stotz and his wife traveled to Havana to talk up the Little League.

In 1952, a team from Montreal, Canada, became the initial non-U.S. team to qualify for the World Series. Peter McGovern, a U.S. Rubber executive, succeeded Carl Stotz as President of the Little League, with Stotz remaining as commissioner and goodwill ambassador. Increasingly, McGovern and his board failed to see eye-to-eye with Stotz on a number of issues. One was expanding the maximum team roster size, which Stotz opposed because it led to diminished playing time for less-talented kids. Stotz also resisted the increasing commercialization of the organization, an indication that if he had remained in charge of Little League, it might have evolved over the subsequent years in a strikingly different manner. The mounting tension ended with Stotz terminating his association with the Little League in 1955.

In 1953, the nationwide appeal of Little League baseball was acknowledged when its World Series final was televised for the first time, with Jim McKay providing the play-by-play for CBS. Red Barber, the Dodgers' colorful play-by-play announcer, provided the commentary for the film CBS produced of the final game.[18]

*

In its initial years, Little League baseball was assumed to be for boys only, with no rule formalizing this understanding deemed necessary. (Carl Stotz, the father of two daughters, admitted in his biography that he regretted not having the time to be able to establish a separate organization for girls.) In 1950, this bastion of maleness was challenged as a result of the determination of thirteen-year-old Kay Johnston. Johnston, who lived in the town of Corning in upstate New York, was athletic and skilled in baseball due to her father's coaching and from competing with boys. "My dad loved baseball," Johnston recalled, "and he was an avid Yankee fan. Many nights, I would sit with him by the radio as he listened to Mel Allen announce games."

Jealous of her younger brother Tom, who was planning to try out for a local Little League team, Johnston cajoled her mother into cutting her braids. Johnston tucked the rest of her hair into a cap, donned one of her brother's T-shirts and a pair of his pants, and rode her bike to the opposite side of town to try out for the Corning Kings Dairy team. She billed herself as "Tubby" Johnston (ironic because she was petite), the alias coming from a boy character in one of her favorite childhood comics, *Little Lulu*.[19] Johnston already was a year over the age limit, but in that time and place, birth certificates weren't checked.

She made the team as a left-handed first baseman. Following several practices and mounting suspicions,

Johnston came clean to her coach. Knowing there was no official rule banning participation by girls, and after asking her teammates for their views, the coach responded, "Well, we all think that if you're good enough to make the team, you're good enough to stay on it." Johnston played the entire season, accepted by her teammates but enduring taunts and boos from opposing players and their parents. "I wasn't trying to be the first at anything," Johnston remembered. "I just wanted to play. It was a wonderful experience—and not only the games themselves. After each one, Mr. King would take us all out for banana splits and milk shakes at his dairy."

Once the season ended, the Little League's reaction was to craft a new rule, commonly referred to as the "Tubby Rule," which officially banned girls from play. That directive stood for more than two decades. In the summer of 1972, when President Richard Nixon signed into law Title IX of the Education Amendments Act prohibiting discrimination on the basis of gender in any federally funded education program or activity, twelve-year-old Maria Pepe of Hoboken, New Jersey, joined a team sponsored by the "Young Democrats" as a pitcher. Her coach, Jimmy Farina, found her baseball prowess to be "exceptional. Better than most of the boys." Pepe herself explained, "I come from a very traditional Italian family, and it shocked my folks that I even wanted to play baseball. But I always thought God gave me certain talents for a reason. Since I played sandlot ball with the boys, why not do so in a uniform?"

Ironically, the town in which Pepe lived arguably is baseball's birthplace. It was in June 1846 on Hoboken's Elysian Fields, across the Hudson River from Manhattan, that the first organized baseball game was believed to have been played between the New York Knickerbocker Baseball Team and the New York Baseball Club.

Hoboken was a fitting locale for a groundbreaking precedent. Moreover, no boys complained about Pepe's presence. However, after Pepe pitched in the season's opening game, several local families, perhaps concerned that a girl might outplay their sons, reported her to the Little League's national office. Per the Tubby Rule, the office demanded that Pepe be removed from the roster, and threatened to revoke Hoboken's charter. Little League senior management warned ominously that enrolling girls "would certainly cripple the program." At a time when more than two million boys globally were playing Little League, Pepe's career was ended after three games.

Pepe's ouster drew the attention of the media and the National Organization for Women, which sued on her behalf. The New Jersey Civil Rights Division sustained Pepe's gender discrimination claim. The case went to the State's highest court, which decided in favor of Pepe in 1974.[20] This time, the League's national office announced that it would "defer to the changing social climate." It determined to not only allow girls to play in its baseball programs but, additionally, to create a softball program for girls only. By the end of that year, nearly 30,000 girls had signed up for softball.

In August 1974, after Nixon resigned from office, the presidency was assumed by Gerald Ford, a former All-Big Ten football player at the University of Michigan who helped the Wolverines to two undefeated seasons and national titles in 1932 and 1933. Ford subscribed to the theory that "there are few things more important to a country's growth and well-being than competitive athletics." In December of that year, he signed into law legislation amending the federal charter for Little League baseball to officially open the program to participation by girls. Three decades later, ESPN would rank Maria Pepe's legal victory as number five on its list of the top ten all-time greatest U.S. women's sports moments.[21]

*

Since Williamsport's founding, there has been a black community in it, and African-American kids have participated in Little League from inception. However, as the organization stretched into the South, it was not immune from the widespread, overt racism infecting the area. In 1955, the year Rosa Parks refused to give up her seat to a white passenger on a Montgomery, Alabama, bus, the all-black Cannon Street YMCA All-Stars of downtown Charleston, walking distance from the city's historic district and within sight of Fort Sumter, where the opening shots of the Civil War were fired, entered the city's Little League tournament. Eight years after Jackie Robinson joined the Brooklyn Dodgers, the Cannon Street team members and coaches embraced the view that baseball would be their path to integration.

That was not to be, as every white team in Charleston refused to play against Cannon Street and the tournament was canceled. To its credit, the national office granted the team permission to compete in the South Carolina State tournament. When all of the state's white-only leagues objected, Little League declared that Cannon Street must be permitted to play, citing bylaws mandating that no individual is to be excluded by reason of race or religion. In response, the South Carolina leagues withdrew from the state tournament, which likewise was canceled.[22] Little League President Peter McGovern lamented, "The Cannon Street players have become innocent victims of alien influences that have deprived them of beneficial associations and the opportunity to meet and know other boys."

Cannon Street was the state champion by default and, therefore, eligible for the South regional tournament to be held in Rome, Georgia, that year, with the winner moving on to the World Series. But the pattern of intolerance held. The regional tournament organizers announced that they would not permit that team to participate because it had advanced by forfeit, a technical decision that McGovern "regretfully" accepted.

As a consolation prize, McGovern invited the Cannon Streeters to be spectators at the World Series, staying in the players' dormitory and eating in their dining facility. The Charleston team made the 740-mile trip in an old school bus that lacked air conditioning, broke down several times, and caught fire a few miles from its destination. Accustomed to state-enforced segregation, the kids were surprised to see other teams' black and white members living in the same quarters and competing against one another. Before the first game, the Cannon Street players were allowed onto the field for batting and fielding practice. When the crowd recognized how talented they were, it began chanting, "Let them play!" To no avail. After watching the final game of that World Series and being recognized with a standing ovation, the team members headed home by bus. On August 28, the day they arrived back in Charleston, Emmett Till, a fourteen-year-old visiting his relatives in Money, Mississippi, was brutalized and murdered after he was accused of offending a white woman, a tragedy that galvanized the press corps and eventually the nation.[23]

*

In 1959, the Little League World Series locale was moved across the river from Original Field to South Williamsport's Howard J. Lamade Memorial Field, which has hosted every championship game since then.[24] Europe first participated in the World Series in 1960, with a team from Berlin being knocked out in the quarterfinal round. By 1962, the World Series truly had gone global, with teams from the Far East also competing for the trip to Williamsport.

In 1963, a team from Granada Hills became the third-straight one from California to win the championship. The final game became a staple for ABC's *Wide World of Sports* program, heralding an explosion of media coverage of the Series.

Coming into the 25th year of Little League play, there were more than 6,500 leagues and 40,000 teams involving more than four million boys in 27 countries.[25] In 1964 alone, almost three times as many Little League games took place than all of the games played over the lifetime of professional baseball. More than 300 former Little Leaguers already had reached the majors, including luminaries such as Joey Jay (the first to become a major-leaguer), Tony Conigliaro, Roger Maris, Boog Powell,[26] and Ron Santo.[27] Two future Presidents (Joe Biden and George W. Bush) and a future Vice President (Dan Quayle) each participated in Little League baseball in the 1950s and credited it with having a major influence on their later successes.

In 1964, a time before the immense growth in the popularity of other professional sports and the explosion of alternate leisure options, as observed by French philosopher and cultural historian Jacques Barzun, baseball ruled the hearts and minds of American boys. Illustrative of this is the comment of Madge Tietz, mother of a 12-year-old boy whose team qualified for Williamsport. "Little League baseball," she said, "is the sun around which his entire universe orbits."

If baseball was religion for boys around the world, then Williamsport was their Bethlehem, Jerusalem, and Mecca rolled into one.

CHAPTER 5
Mid-Island Little League

Coach Rogers was a true field general who pushed his young players toward perfection. Yet he knew when to back off and show the other side of his personality, which resembled Yogi Bear—kind and tolerant.

—Eddie Godnig

In 1953, Christopher (Buddy) Cusack, while attending Golden Gloves boxing matches for boys, reflected on the lack of similar availability of youth baseball competition on the Island. After purchasing a wetland plot in Dongan Hills, near South Beach, Cusack and several friends labored for months to create a Little League playing field.[28] They received critical assistance from the new borough president, Albert Maniscalco, who was known for going out of his way for constituents. "Many years later," Jay Price recalled, "I was sitting next to Maniscalco at a civic event. He told me that, to help out Cusack, he had directed an extensive operation that diverted City trucks and drivers to scour the Island for dirt and fill to dump into the marsh. Then he whispered to me, 'If any of that story ever got out, I'd have gone to jail.'"

Leagues sprang up all over Staten Island. The Mid-Island Little League, formed in 1956, was aptly named, being located in the midst of the East Shore, Great Kills, North Shore, South Shore, and West Shore leagues.

In 1964, the MILL majors season (for eleven- and twelve-year-old boys) commenced in March with tryouts for those who lived in the interconnected neighborhoods of Bulls Head, Castleton Corners, Manor Heights, Meiers Corners, Sunnyside, and Westerleigh.[29] "Back then," Jeff Paul explained, "when they held tryouts, they'd put an index card with a number on your shirt held with a safety pin. Your number was called when it was your turn to do something. Then, you were assigned to a team, hopefully with some of your buddies. It was an old-school system, but it worked." Each boy was evaluated based on his ability to hit, field, throw, and run the bases, with managers looking for skills, speed, quickness, arm strength, and a positive, enthusiastic attitude.

After tryouts came draft night, when the members of each team were selected by managers. Each squad was assigned a draft slot dictated by the League standings of the previous year, with the champions picking last.

MILL home games were played at Cascio Field, a baseball outpost now lost to urban development that had been situated below Victory Boulevard on Richmond Avenue in Bulls Head. "There was a real baseball feel to Cascio," Paul recalled. "Well-kept field. Electric scoreboard. Ten-foot-high fences. Classy dugouts. And it was rustic, surrounded by creeks, open fields, and marshes. Right behind the field was a flowing stream, known as the Great Swamp Ditch, that kids would float down on rafts and skate on in the winter."

Pat Salmon, the author of several books on the history of Staten Island, was four years old in 1964. She came of age in Bulls Head. "There were farms that covered a few dozen acres each, operated mostly by Italian and Greek immigrants. Some included orchards where grapes were grown, stomped, and left to ferment in giant tubs. On one farm near us, there was a hutch of rabbits. I thought the animals were being kept as pets, not realizing they were there to be turned into stew. Houses that weren't farms typically grew vegetables and flowers for sale in their front yard."

When Salmon was growing up, there were few organized activities for kids. "Everyone always complained," she recollected, "that there was nothing going on and nothing for us to do. My family lived a short walk from Cascio Field. So if there was a Little League game on a Friday or Saturday evening, often the entire family went. The one problem was that the marshes drew swarms of mosquitoes. Sometimes, when we played there, we'd gather and burn cattails to keep the bugs away."[30]

In 1964, MILL was composed of six teams, with a volunteer coach and assistant coach for each. The league was fortunate to have quality coaches, for teaching proficiency is acutely important when managing eleven- and twelve-year-old boys still learning a complex sport that requires at its higher levels mastering innumerable skills. Teaching Little Leaguers is further demanding because they're developing physically, socially, emotionally, and cognitively. At that age, some may have passed puberty while other are in it or rapidly approaching. Ideally, coaches also help every kid in their care to appreciate the importance of the "intangibles" such as hard work, focus, teamwork, and sportsmanship.

One of the six MILL teams, Aliseo Brothers' Meat Market, was coached by Bill Rogers. A tough-looking, snub-nosed redhead who stood six feet two inches and weighed 235 pounds, Rogers was born and raised in Westerleigh, the neighborhood south of Port Richmond. He was a stellar athlete who'd played varsity baseball and basketball at Port Richmond High School. An only child, Rogers told his parents James and Letty that he was so perfect they didn't need another kid. "My dad agreed. My mom, not so much."

Rogers was talented enough in basketball to be offered a college scholarship in the sport. But baseball was his great passion, so he instead joined the Washington Senators' farm system in Erie, Pennsylvania (1953) and Hagerstown, Pennsylvania (1954), as a third baseman playing in the Pennsylvania-Ontario-New York League. After two years, Rogers gave up the dream. "I was good defensively. I just couldn't hit well enough."

After Rogers returned home, his father, a manager at Procter & Gamble's Ivory Soap factory in Port Ivory, a coastal area in the northwestern corner of the Island, found him a job there.[31] "It was hard manual work. I'd spend hours each day loading big wooden trays of soap."

In 1956, a friend told Rogers about the new MILL league. He volunteered as a coach for a minor league team and, in his first year of managing, won his division. The following year, Rogers was entrusted with a major league team and, at the end of the regular season, was picked to be assistant coach for the MILL All-Star team that competed in Little League World Series tournament play.

By 1958, in view of his demonstrated coaching prowess and high-level playing background (among Little League managers, minor league experience is the equivalent of a baseball Ph.D.), Rogers was offered the position of coaching MILL's All-Stars. He was only 23 years old, and several fathers questioned the wisdom of that decision. All objections abated when Rogers proceeded to lead the All-Star team to the New York City championships and win it, the first time a Staten Island team had done so.[32]

Leo Durocher, the legendary although controversial baseball manager, snidely observed, "Baseball is like church. Many attend, but few understand." Rogers clearly understood. His subsequent decades of coaching success derived from his deep knowledge of the intricacies of baseball and ability to convey them. Also, and in spite of a forceful personality, Rogers was adept at social interactions and building relationships with other coaches, parents, umpires, and league officials. For a Little League coach, effective communication with parents is critical, as they are entrusting him with their precious children's development both as ballplayers and persons. Rogers demonstrated his skill at doing so while treating their sons with respect. Rogers, in turn, earned widespread respect. "A lot of parents," Paul noted, "called him 'Mr. Rogers,' even though he was more than a decade younger than most of them."

Over the decades, a persistent criticism of Little League is that it overemphasizes the importance of winning at the potential expense of other qualities such as sportsmanship and building character. Those critics might have had a bone to pick with Rogers, who possessed a fiercely competitive drive. The willingness to compete, particularly against strong opponents, is essential to a successful athlete and team and best developed at a young age. Rogers issued to his players no bromides such as, "Try your best and you will have succeeded" or "It's not whether you win or lose, it's how you play the game." He set high standards for himself and imparted them onto his players.

Due in large part to Rogers, in the early 1960s, MILL was the dominant league not only on Staten Island, a hotbed of baseball, but in all the City. In 1962, Rogers' All-Star team again captured the New York City Little League championship. A year later, Rogers held high hopes for his squad, which was loaded with talent, including three starters near six feet tall. The standout was Peter Wyso, a switch hitter who could drive the ball 300 feet from either side of the plate. "Wyso," Joe Nugent recounted, "must have hit thirty to forty home runs in regular-season play in 1963. He got so bored smashing them right handed that he switched to batting left handed. If he got the ball up in the air, you assumed it would go over the fence. There was no one on the 1964 team with raw hitting ability anywhere close to Wyso's."[33]

In 1963, MILL secured the Staten Island Little League championship in dramatic fashion against West Shore, an adjacent league that was its greatest rival, when Billy Ebner, one of four eleven-year-olds on that team, hit a grand slam in the bottom of the sixth for the only runs scored in the game. Then MILL cruised to the New York City championship, crushing its finals opponent 18–1. It was the first time a league had won the City title two years in a row. Reaching Williamsport and the World Series appeared quite possible.

In its semifinal game of the Eastern Regionals against Connellsville, Pennsylvania, MILL enjoyed home-field advantage. The game was played on a Thursday evening at Hy Turkin Memorial Field in Dongan Hills, and the stands were packed with 5,000 rabid fans. (Turkin was a prominent New York City sportswriter, best known for co-editing the first baseball encyclopedia, who passed away at age 40.) Wyso was MILL's pitcher that day, and he was throwing "aspirin tablets," as was the Connellsville starter.[34]

MILL went ahead early in the game by one run. Feeling the tension was shortstop Johnny Currado, one of the starting eleven-year-olds. Fun-loving but intense, Currado obsessed about baseball, honing his skills even in the winter by throwing a ball in his backyard garage. Currado's lineage on both sides was Italian, with all four grandparents coming through Ellis Island. (Italian-Americans were so prevalent on Staten Island that the borough garnered the nickname

"Staten Italy.") His father was an insurance salesman for Met Life but, as was the case with many dads of that era, took on other work as well. One undertaking was in the Island's Gold Seal ice cream factory. "My father worked in the freezer for hours stacking cartons of ice cream before the trucks picked them up. Obviously, working in the cold was real tough. He also tended bar when he could. Dad was always hustling to support my two sisters, my brother, and me."

Currado arguably was ineligible to play on the MILL team. "I was born and raised in Mariners Harbor on the north shore, near the Bayonne Bridge, a mostly Italian, Irish, and Polish middle-class melting pot. My uncle, an ex-minor league baseball player who taught me the game, coached a MILL team. He got me into that league when I was six. So although we remained living in Mariners Harbor, outside the district, I was grandfathered into MILL because I'd played there for years."

In the top of the sixth, a Connellsville batter reached second base with two outs. The next batter slammed a ground ball at Currado. It went through his legs, and the runner scored, tying the game. "I was inconsolable, feeling I'd let everyone down," Currado remembered. "It took me a while to get over that mistake, even though Coach Rogers kept telling me that one player doesn't lose a game."

In the bottom of the sixth, with two out, there were MILL runners on first and second. "Wyso, our big hitter," Rogers recalled, "belted a shot to right center. I jumped up, ready to celebrate, but their right fielder made a great play, leaping above the fence to catch the ball and end the inning."

The game continued into extra innings. In the top of the ninth, with a runner on second base and two outs, the Connellsville batter lined a ball over first base down the right field line, where Greg Klee was playing. "I corralled the ball quickly and fired it to Wyso, the cutoff man on that play. We had the runner dead to rights, but Pete was a bit out of position and when he turned, in his hurry to get the runner, he threw the ball past Kevin Hurley, our catcher. That allowed what proved to be the winning run to score."

The Connellsville game was burned into the memories of the MILL boys who played in it. That stinging loss proved to be a fierce, invaluable motivation throughout the following year's tournament.

CHAPTER 6
The Pieces Fall Into Place

Danny was twelve going on seventeen. He already had a Dean Martin suave personality.

—Joe Nugent

IN MID-JUNE 1964, after the regular season ended, Rogers and the managers of the other five teams that comprised MILL met at Cascio Field to decide on the best fourteen players in the league, who would form the All-Star team. (In addition to the fourteen boys selected for this team, there were two "alternates" named who would have joined the team had a player gotten injured or otherwise not been able to travel to games.)

Rogers chose three boys from his own team. One was Greg Klee. Gangly ("you could count my ribs without me holding my breath"), with a mouthful of braces and a happy-go-lucky personality, he was the second child in a family of seven. Klee's mother, Rosemary, was a full-blooded Italian-American who joked about the fact that she was born on

St. Patrick's Day. Rosemary was a stay-at-home mom until her youngest turned ten. Then she returned to school for a nursing degree and found employment at Staten Island Hospital.

Klee's dad, Bob, of Dutch-German heritage, taught Greg baseball. "He caught my throws," Greg described, "with an old brown glove that was as big as a pillow, like the ones players used early in the century." Bob Klee worked for the New York City Transit Authority and also took on other jobs, at times holding three at once, as Johnny Currado's father did. Notwithstanding his heavy workload, Bob Klee found the time to manage the Art Foley's Gulf MILL team. Bucking tradition, he avoided selecting his son for that team, feeling it would be best for Greg to play for and learn from another coach. "That led," Greg Klee recalled, "to a friendly but passionate competition between us."

Bob Klee was more outwardly cheerful and laid-back than Rogers. But he knew baseball, took coaching seriously, and bonded well with his players, several of the reasons why Rogers chose him to be the assistant coach for the MILL All-Star team. "Bob was not only a good coach," Rogers stated, "he was a friend and a man I admired."

As Greg Klee explained, "Coach Rogers intuitively understood that he and my dad would complement each other well. And that was true to a greater extent than Rogers even realized. Because while he personified our team, my dad, an only child who never had the chance to play an organized amateur sport, truly lived vicariously through us kids. He became as much a part of our Little League team as a middle-aged man could have been."

The two other boys chosen for the All-Star team by Rogers from his Aliseo Brothers roster each had played for him for two years. One was Eddie Godnig Jr., who grew up with an older and a younger sister on Drake Avenue in Castleton Corners. Godnig's maternal grandparents had emigrated from Sicily, and his father's father from Trieste, when it was within the Austro-Hungarian Empire. Godnig's father, Edward Senior, served in the U.S. Air Force during World War II. A year after the war ended, Godnig's parents wed and set up their home on Staten Island, where his mother, Mary, had been born and raised. With the help of the GI Bill, Ed Godnig Senior studied to become an aeronautic design engineer, ultimately working for Fairchild Hiller Aviation.

"As a kid, life was sweet and simple," Godnig recounted. "My house was a stone's throw from Clove Lakes Park, an oasis of interconnected lakes and ponds surrounded by woods and bordering the Staten Island Zoo. You could do a lot in that park. Baseball, basketball, fishing, skating, and more. We also were right near the New York Armory off of Manor Road, which had a large field that kids would sneak into. I spent most of my time playing in a five-square-block area. We rarely left the Island. A really big deal was the occasional trip on the ferry to 'the City.'"

When Godnig was eight, like many of the boys in his neighborhood, he embarked on his Little League career in the MILL Farm League, where his father was a coach. "My dad built a pitching mound and home plate in our side yard so that we could practice together. Being a meticulous engineer, Dad made sure they were exactly 46 feet apart, in line with Little League dimensions. It was so much fun trying to knock him over with my fastballs."

The other Aliseo Brothers team member selected by Rogers was Dominic "Donny" Quattrochi, born in a heavily Italian-American Port Richmond section of the Island on the north shore across from Bayonne, New Jersey. Quattrochi in Italian means "four eyes." "How our family got its name," Quattrochi explained, "is a mystery and for a long time has been the subject of a lot of fun speculation."

Quattrochi's family moved to Westerleigh when he was a toddler. His mother, Dolly, was a homemaker who at times waitressed at a local pizzeria. His father, Philip, a World War II Navy veteran, had emigrated from Corleone, Sicily, where his family members were sheepherders. In one of innumerable examples over the course of U.S. history of how baseball unites native and immigrant, Philip Quattrochi came to love the sport and to imbue that passion into his son.

As Donny describes it, his family life was "very regimented. You didn't get nothing for nothing. You had to do chores like cleaning your room. When I was ten, I was given a paper route, and then my dad got me an after-school job stocking shelves at a local deli. Once I was paid, I would leave the cash on the kitchen table along with a note to my mom saying, 'Here's my money. Love, Donny.' I was raised to do what was right. The worst thing I remember us kids doing was going into the woods to smoke cigarettes."

In addition to Greg Klee, Rogers also brought back the other three eleven-year-old boys who had played on his 1963 All-Star team—Currado, Ebner, and Danny Yaccarino. Yaccarino was yet another team member with Italian heritage on both sides, his four grandparents having emigrated from Naples. Yaccarino's paternal grandfather set up on Staten Island a *mercarto* (market), in his case, a fruit stand, a traditional occupation for Italian immigrants in the early 20th century.

Yaccarino, only 5'3" and barely more than a hundred pounds with glove and uniform, was a gifted athlete with a lightning fastball and superb control who also played a solid second base and hit well. Moreover, Yaccarino possessed other, more intangible qualities. Whether at an amateur or professional level, a manager can push his team members only so much. Motivation must come from the players as well, and Yaccarino, brash and confident, was a natural clubhouse leader.

Three additional boys, none of whom had played for Rogers before, became key ingredients of this All-Star team. One was Bobby Nugent, who played for R.G. Jacobson Ace's Hardware. Like Yaccarino, Nugent was cocky and outspoken. He also was a class clown, invariably searching for the humor in any situation.

Nugent grew up with three siblings in Manor Heights, situated down the hill from the ritzy Todt Hill neighborhood famous for two reasons. One is that it contains the highest natural point not only in New York City but throughout the Atlantic Coast south of Maine, at a measly 401 feet above sea level. The other is serving at the time as the home location of several Mafia bosses and drug kingpins. Indeed, adjoining Todt Hill is the Emerson Hill locale, used for filming the Don Corleone compound scenes in the *Godfather* movies.

Yaccarino's and Nugent's houses sat back to back on Mountainview Avenue. "We played a lot together," Nugent recollected. "Whiffle ball, stickball, basketball, and pitching cards in our backyards or the schoolyard." Nugent's father, Joseph Senior, a Navy veteran, was a Brooklyn Dodgers fan who soured on the team after it left the City for Los Angeles in 1957. "My dad became a Yankee fan and turned me and my brother Joe into rabid ones. Whitey Ford and Mickey Mantle were my idols. I lived and died with Mantle's at bats. And Yankee Stadium was a temple to me. One day, when I was only ten, I took the R6 bus by myself to the Staten Island ferry. On the Manhattan side, I hopped on the D train and rode it to Yankee Stadium, where I paid fifty cents to watch a high school all-star game. A kid could do things like that in those days."

Richie Smiechowski, thin, shy, and a bundle of energy, was the only eleven-year-old chosen for the All-Star team. Smiechowski grew up in the Sunnyside neighborhood along with an older brother and two younger sisters. "It was a wonderful place," he reminisced. "We were surrounded by parks, the schools were great, and I had tons of friends. I feel blessed that my parents had the foresight to choose to live in Staten Island."

Chapter 6

Then there was Jeff Paul, who played on Bob Klee's
team during the regular season. In the Paul household,
as in millions of others across the nation and generations,
the deep emotional commitment between father and son
intertwined with their mutual love of baseball. "When I was
six," Paul recalled, "my dad took me to a game at Ebbets
Field. I remember, as we entered, staring at the white marble
rotunda and the huge chandelier with twelve baseball bat
arms holding baseball lamps. Then I saw the field and was
blown away."

At an early age, Lawrence Paul taught his son baseball in nearby Clove Lakes Park, which was dotted with
playgrounds, athletic fields, and baseball diamonds. As
with Godnig, after Jeff Paul joined Little League as an
eight-year-old, his father, upon hearing that his son would
be doing some pitching, built a mound in their backyard,
paced off 46 feet, and laid down a home plate. "He'd come
home from work and within minutes I'd be throwing to him.
He'd spend hours of his spare time each weekend teaching
me to pitch and catching me."

The membership of the 1964 MILL All-Star team now
decided, Rogers phoned the parents of the boys chosen.
Over a half century later, while recounting the moment
he learned he'd been selected, Paul choked with emotion.
"I walked into my house. Mom and Dad were at the top of
the landing. Mom had a sheepish grin while Dad kept a
poker face. 'We just got a phone call from Bill Rogers,' he
said in a serious tone. I began to panic, trying to figure out
what bad thing I might have done. Then Dad smiled and

told me I had been selected for the All-Star team. Both of them hugged me. It's a moment that has stayed with me my entire life."

CHAPTER 7
Carnegie Hall

We ran laps until our tongues hung out. Like we were in the Army. I told people that my manager was trying to kill us.

—Greg Klee

AFTER DRAFT NIGHT, Rogers met with the sixteen boys chosen to be on the MILL All-Star team and their parents. He laid out his program, rules, and expectation of total commitment by each adult and child. Parents were to ensure their son attended every practice and game and that he arrive on time. "If anyone's going on vacation," I told them, "you can go. But your kid stays home. If he goes with you, he's no longer on the team."

Rogers banned other sports during that summer, including swimming. "I basically told the dads and moms," he confessed, "that their child was mine for the next two months. To their credit, while some may not have been very happy about that, no one complained. Success in the tournament depended on their active cooperation, and

*Top row, from left, Bill Rogers, Jeff Paul, Bobby Nugent,
Greg Klee, Gary Kresge, Danny Yaccarino, Frankie Higgins,
Donny Quattrochi, Billy Ebner, John Porcell, and Bob Klee.
Bottom row, from left, David Intartaglia, Steve Schaffer,
Johnny Currado, Richie Smiechowski, Mickey Wicinski, Mike
Troiano, and Eddie Godnig. Intartaglia and Schaffer were
alternates who never joined the team during the tournament.*

they gave me that. The parents, including mine, ended up
enjoying that summer as much as the kids did. And they
all became close. I never sensed any animosity."

Rogers was entitled to only two weeks of vacation from
work, but many additional days would be required that summer. "The Procter & Gamble people," Rogers explained,
"were very good about allowing me leave on tournament
days. Of course, it was without pay."

The parents sacrificed as well. They were middle class, largely living paycheck to paycheck, with little extra money for the travel and hotel expenses that mounted as the team's success swelled. Yet most found the time and means to serve an integral role in their sons' special summer. Joe and Bobby Nugent's father was a captain in the New York Fire Department. "In those days," Joe noted, "it wasn't easy for a fireman to switch around his scheduled time. Dad needed to swap shifts, what they call getting 'mutuals.' All of which had to be paid back after the season was over. But he made it work."

Rogers' message to his team was direct. Williamsport was the goal. "He assured us," Donny Quattrochi remembered, "that we had the talent to get to the World Series and that we would achieve that if we worked hard enough. And we believed him." Danny Yaccarino recalled, "Coach Rogers was godlike to me. Once he said that to us, I never doubted that we would make it to Williamsport and win it all."

During that initial meeting and throughout the summer, when Rogers spoke, the boys listened. Greg Klee admitted that, "If Coach Rogers told us to jump, we asked, 'How high?'" As Quattrochi made clear, "We all were very much raised to respect our elders. But there were other factors. One was a touch of fear. Coach Rogers was big and intimidating, with Popeye arms and a stern voice. But even more than that, he commanded our attention because we understood, even at an early age, that he had a terrific baseball mind."

*

The 1964 MILL All-Star team has been portrayed as a "machine." How did that come to be? The answer is the same as for the classic joke about a tourist in Manhattan asking a passerby how to get to Carnegie Hall. "Practice, practice, practice."

Rogers believed in the principle articulated by renowned basketball coach Bobby Knight that, "The key is not the will to win... everybody has that. It is the will to prepare to win that's important." As Eddie Godnig noted, "Coach Rogers not only had a natural talent for coaching baseball, but he was a master motivator and psychologist. And it all revolved around his intense daily practices." Jay Price commented that Rogers' 1964 practice regimen "was far advanced, certainly for players of that age."

Rogers' plan was to mold the boys into a tightly knit, self-assured band of brothers. Unlike a sport such as basketball, where the ball can be placed in the hands of the best scorer one possession after another, baseball players come to bat once every nine times and can only play one position on the field at a time. Consequently, a complete team effort is necessary to win consistently in baseball at a high level.

There was limited time to prepare for tournament play. Until school ended in late June, the boys worked out at Cascio Field each weekday following classes until dark and twice a day on weekends. As soon as the school year ended, Rogers ran the team through two practices a day. He broke down the elements of play into their basics, demonstrated them, and instilled those abilities into the boys through intensive drills until they were flawless and instinctive. Every area, including baserunning, sliding, hitting, fielding, and throwing, was covered, with no facet of the game being too insignificant for Rogers to address. "Coach Rogers," Yaccarino remembered, "even designed our uniforms and taught us the correct way of putting them on."

The first daily session started at 8 a.m. sharp and lasted until noon, with water and snack breaks. Anyone who arrived late was required to run laps. As mornings were cooler, after stretching legs and hamstrings and warming up arms, the focus was on fielding, pitching, and running the bases. Rogers taught his boys skills such as managing a rundown, sliding into a bag while escaping being tagged, fielding the ball cleanly, and gripping the ball correctly before a throw. During each practice, an infielder would handle more than a hundred ground balls.

Outfielders similarly would catch dozens of fly balls plus work on cutoffs, used when a ball is hit to the outfield and a runner attempts to advance to another base. Cutoffs avoid outfielders having to make a long throw by themselves, a task difficult for Little Leaguers. Rogers emphasized the need to throw straight and accurately on a line low enough for the infielder to easily catch the ball and turn. MILL's mastery of cutoff throws proved to be one of the reasons for its success, as it saved multiple runs during tournament play.

The boys were allowed an hour for lunch at the field, eating food brought from home or bought from the snack bar. The afternoon session, which started at one p.m. and continued to five p.m., was devoted to hitting. Rogers stressed fundamentals such as lower- and upper-body position and movement, reading the type of pitch and where it will end up in relation to the batter's box, awareness of the strike zone, swinging the hips around until the body is square, where to stand in the batter's box, how to hold the bat, and getting a jump out of the batter's box.

Over the years, the long ball has proven to be the magic elixir for many Little League championship teams. Rogers recognized that his 1964 team on average was not as big and strong as that of his previous year and wasn't going to win games via the long ball. They would need to excel at pitching, defense, and small ball, meaning getting runners on base and advancing them with bunts, stolen bases, and sacrifice flies.

This approach jived with Rogers' penchant to think like a chess player with an array of tactics available to him. One was the ready ability of his players to bunt, whether as a sacrifice or to reach base. Rogers demonstrated to his kids how to deaden the ball by allowing it to strike a still bat held at the top of the strike zone with bended legs. "Coach Rogers," Richie Smiechowski recalled, "believed strongly in preparation to minimize what was left to chance. There was no area that he applied this to more than bunting, and it became clear during the tournament that we were better at that than any team we faced. In fact, some teams didn't seem to know how to bunt at all. That gave us a huge advantage."

Certain days, based on the energy of the players, Rogers would extend practice until dark. "If there wasn't enough light to take at-bats, we held sliding practice," Bobby Nugent recollected. "When Coach Rogers first told us to do a hook slide, I had no idea what it was."

Most of the time, drills were being conducted all over the field, requiring Rogers to enlist help in supervising them. A key assistant was Mike Sosa, coach of a MILL minor league team at the time. Sosa, born in East Harlem, had a baseball background having been the catcher on a Manhattan High School of Aviation Trades varsity team that featured, as its number one pitcher, Whitey Ford.

The Sosa and Yaccarino families lived around the block from each other and were close, which led Sosa to meet Rogers and eventually form a friendship. Sosa attended most of the MILL All-Star practices and became an unofficial second assistant coach.

Rogers also enlisted the help of several fathers glad to be involved whenever they were able to find time away from work. One was Phil Ebner, who worked at the Piels Brewery.[35] He became the regular batting-practice hurler and a special part of MILL's success. "I'm not sure how he did it," Billy Ebner recalled, "but my dad not only came to every game but also to most every practice. They called him 'Iron Mike' because he could throw strikes for hours. Watching my dad work with our team and seeing him cheer us on are among my fondest memories. It's the reason I felt so strongly about coaching each of my four daughters in softball and making it to their games."

Phil Ebner was a bear of a man, and that, too, brought its benefits. "Standing up against a large man like Mr. Ebner," Godnig explained, "gave us confidence that we could certainly hang tough against smaller Little League pitchers."

Fathers weren't the only ones pressed into service by Rogers. Joe Nugent, a former MILL All-Star himself, was fifteen at the time. "One day, Coach Rogers asked me to come over and pitch batting practice. I was in high school then and afraid that, standing only 46 feet away, I might throw a wild pitch and break someone's bone or worse. I told Rogers that, and he responded, 'Don't worry. Just throw as hard as you can.'"

Yogi Berra once observed, "Baseball is ninety percent mental. The other half is physical." Rogers continuously reminded, "Do not beat yourself!" As Currado described, "In the field, we knew where to go when the ball was hit. At bat, we always had a plan to execute based on the situation. On the bases, we never ran ourselves into outs." Rogers also stressed the importance of a player's awareness of the game circumstances before each pitch, such as number of outs, how many runners on and where, the score, who's batting, and whether it's a bunt situation, and thus knowing exactly what to do if the ball comes his way. And Rogers taught that there's usually something a player can do on every play even if the ball isn't hit to him, such as backing up a throw or covering a base.

Rogers constantly preached that "fewest mistakes wins games." "If one of my kids screwed up," Rogers recounted with a smile, "like throwing to the wrong base or being in the incorrect position for a cutoff, he would look at me nervously because he knew I'd be unhappy. What I wanted each of them to understand was more than that screwups are bad. It was that, as in life, luck is an essential and unpredictable reality of baseball. Like a swing meant to be checked that bloops the ball just over the infield or a long fly ball that a sudden wind pushes fair or foul. You're gonna get your share of bad luck, and you can't control that. What you can manage and you must manage is eliminating your mental errors."

The penalty for a gaffe by a MILL team member, whether poor execution or lack of energy or focus, was running laps around the field. No one was spared. "What made it even worse," Greg Klee said with a chuckle, "was that, while we were running, Coach Rogers would sit in the dugout with a cold drink. I always was cursing and bitching during those laps, but I had to whisper my complaints. It was hard for others to hear me, which is why I got the nickname 'Mumbles.'"

The value of constant communication was reinforced by Rogers. He expected his players to shout the number of outs after one was recorded, call fly balls, yell out instructions on cutoffs and bases to throw to, and remind others of who covers on a steal or where to throw to on an infield grounder with runners on base. "One day," Currado remembered, "it was really hot, and we infielders were not chatting it up enough, which Coach Rogers wanted us to do to show enthusiasm and send a message to our opponent that we were prepared and ready to go. He stopped practice in the middle of a drill, called the team to the dugout, glared at us with his classic disappointed look, and barked, "Twenty laps!" Normally, it was ten laps for a mistake, so I was thinking, *He won't make us run twenty laps.* Boy was I wrong. We all started to jog around the field when the call came to "pick it up!" Everyone completed the twenty laps, and our reward was a drink of Orangeade and back out on the field with the same drill."

Richie Smiechowski's memories revolve around the practices more than the games. "Apart from all the laps we did for screwing up, we'd always end the day with a series of wind sprints that pushed the young bodies to the brink of exhaustion. We did those no matter how hot it was or how long a day we'd had."

Rogers often treated his kids as if they possessed the physical abilities of an adult. Bobby Nugent recalled, "Coach Rogers would come out with a fungo bat, take two steps up, and smash grounders at me at the hot corner that I had to get in front of. And I was less than 60 feet away. That did two things. For me, it gave me a lot of faith in my fielding ability during a game because I knew that nobody playing Little League could hit a ball that hard. And when he would do that same thing during drills before a game, it would demoralize the other team."

Rogers mixed strict discipline with constant support and encouragement. "One word of recognition from him," Godnig admitted, "would pick up our spirits and make us feel we were capable of accomplishing greatness." And he led by example. "Coach Rogers," Jeff Paul observed, "worked longer hours and with more intensity than any of us. And the team took on his work ethic."

To a man, the players' memories of those practices are fond ones. "Despite the heat and the laps and the scrutiny, " Danny Yaccarino said, "nobody wanted to stop." But Yaccarino and the others note that what also made the punishing practices pleasant was the presence of the assistant coach, Bob Klee. "Greg's dad," Paul recounted, "was a fair and funny man, even-keeled, and a straight shooter. He was a home run." As Smiechowski described, "Coach Klee was a wonderful first lieutenant, and our buffer. When Rogers would yell at me, Klee would come over, put his arm around me, and say 'Richie, don't worry about it. Just think about what you did wrong and then go back out there and keep hustling and make sure to do it right the next time.' He and Rogers had a good cop, bad cop routine that worked well." Nugent characterized Coach Klee as the constant calming presence for the team. "He would tell me, 'C'mon, Nuge, let me hear you smile.' On the bus, he would lead us in singing songs. He understood that we were still boys."

By the end of the weeks of practice, Rogers had imparted a set of skills and a strategic understanding of the game far advanced from those possessed by most other teams. Yet another attribute inculcated in that MILL squad was emotional toughness, an essential feature for any team seeking a championship in high-level competition. "You only get such resilience," Rogers explained, "through purposeful training and repetition. Which leads to knowing what you need to do in every situation without having to think much about it."

*

As men nearing their 70s, the members of the 1964 MILL team still spoke of Rogers with reverence, granting him a majority of the credit for their championship as well as part of the reason for their professional and personal achievements as adults. "Coach Rogers and his practices," Currado observed, "taught me the importance of diligent preparation. To not take shortcuts and rely just on talent, but to do the dirty work. To withstand disappointments and to use constructive feedback from others. To never show up late for an appointment or meeting. To believe that I could accomplish anything I put my mind to achieve."

CHAPTER 8
The 12-6

In those days, few Little League batters could hit a good curveball, even if they were expecting it. And it's near impossible for a batter looking for a curve ball to hit a good fastball."

— Bill Rogers

AS BOYS WERE PICKED from various MILL teams to be All-Stars based on talent, Rogers needed to decide position after the fact. Initially, it was assumed that Greg Klee and Billy Ebner, big, strong lefty hurlers, would be the starting pitchers. But Klee had thrown his arm out during regular season play. (Little League would later implement a per-game pitch-count limit to help prevent this problem.) During All-Star competition the previous year, Rogers had played Klee in right field and, now, given his speed and range, he shifted him to center field. Ebner, who likewise was having troubles with his pitching arm, was assigned to first base, where he proved to be solid defensively. "Billy,"

Eddie Godnig recounted, "scooped up everything you threw at him."

Even if the arms of Ebner and Klee were healthy, the two remained with a distinct disadvantage, because they couldn't throw a curveball well. And to Bill Rogers, that consideration was of paramount importance.

The discovery in 1873 of the curveball, a wonder of physics, transformed the game. The man credited with inventing the pitch is Candy Cummings, who, as a fourteen-year-old, developed the idea while throwing clamshells into the ocean at a Brooklyn beach. After causing the shells to fly in wide arcs based on their shape and the method in which he hurled them, Cummings recognized that he could apply the same principles to throwing a baseball, by gripping and releasing the ball in a way that not only causes a forward trajectory but, also, imbues it with spin. Cummings found through experimentation that a sharp vertical break is created when the pitcher's forearm and wrist twist, like yanking a doorknob while throwing, before the ball is released. The diminutive Cummings' invention of the curveball helped him to enjoy a successful, albeit brief, career as a pitcher and led him to be inducted into the Baseball Hall of Fame.[36]

As innumerable children and men have learned over the subsequent century and a half, including world-class athletes like Michael Jordan, it's difficult to hit a curveball. The batter needs to hesitate and keep his hands and weight back in order to allow the ball to come to him. Otherwise, he's hitting off his front foot. And depending on which grip and motion the pitcher uses, the ball, at differing speeds, will turn down, down and away, or down and in. Thus, it's challenging to make the split-second guess as to the ball's ending-up point. Over the years, the option of throwing a curveball brought a higher level of strategy into the game, even in Little League.

To Rogers' mind, his team would not be successful if its pitchers were limited to fastballs. A batter expecting a heater has a better chance of timing it well than a batter who isn't sure what pitch will be thrown. Supplementing the arsenal of a hard-throwing pitcher with a curveball exponentially increases his advantage against a batter. As baseball legend Hank Aaron once said, "Guessing what the pitcher is going to throw is eighty percent of being a successful hitter. The other twenty percent is just execution."

Danny Yaccarino could throw a fabulous curveball. His father had been an Army staff sergeant who strived to be perfect in everything he did. That attitude rubbed off on his son, who would spend hours a day throwing a Spaldeen against the steps of his house. "I developed a curveball, and I got to the point where I could hit precise spots on the steps with different pitches to create any type of line drive, fly ball, or ground ball. That contributed to my control. Sometimes though, I'd miss, and my mom would come out and yell at me to stop."

If Rogers' masterful coaching was the primary reason for MILL's championship season, a close second was his decision to name Yaccarino the number-one starting pitcher. During the 1964 regular Little League season, Yaccarino played for the Northfield (Savings Bank) Sabers. At the end of that season, and after the MILL All-Star team had been selected, Northfield faced off against Rogers' Aliseo Brothers' team for the title. Yaccarino, the starting pitcher, got hit hard, and Northfield lost. When Rogers shook Danny's hand following the game, the sullen twelve-year-old told him, "Don't count on me as your pitcher. Pick someone else." Rogers responded, "No, you'll be fine—don't worry about it."

Rogers named Yaccarino the All-Star team's number-one pitcher, with Jeff Paul and Bobby Nugent, each of whom had pitched a no-hitter during the regular season, as the other starters. Rogers would take the three boys aside during each morning practice and work with them, helping to establish consistent mechanics, including proper balance, knee lift, stride length, and follow-through. He made clear to them that, in addition to spin and speed, the release point of the curveball is key to its effectiveness. "When you throw a curveball," Rogers clarified, "the trick is to pick out a target on the catcher, like his eyes, nose, or chin, and then picture yourself handing him the ball at that spot. That's where you turn the wrist, with your hand coming down to the left ankle on the follow through." Rogers' goal was to have each pitcher be able to consistently throw both a curveball and a fastball with speed, movement, and pinpoint location. "I would tell each of my pitchers to 'just miss,' and they could do that," Rogers explained.

It may appear redundant to speak of a fastball as having "movement," but not all fastballs are alike. Yaccarino could throw a "two-seamer," a slightly slower variant of a straight or "four-seam" fastball. A four-seam grip, meaning holding the ball so that both the index and middle fingers are touching two seams perpendicularly, eliminates movement to the sides and forces the ball into a straight downward trajectory as opposed to sailing, which bolsters accuracy.

In contrast, a two-seam fastball is thrown by placing the index and middle fingers on the ball where the seams are closest together, with the thumb resting underneath. The ball moves several inches down and in the same direction as whichever arm is being used to throw it, meaning a right-handed pitcher gets rightward break on a two-seamer. The degree of drop of a two-seam fastball depends on the arm slot angle and finger pressure used. Because it's complex to throw, the pitch is more difficult to master and control. "In a fastball situation," Yaccarino clarified, "I'd mainly use a two-seamer as it had pretty good tail. I'd shift to the four-seamer if I needed to make sure I threw a strike."

As for Yaccarino's curveball, Rogers was concerned that his three-quarters delivery, in which the ball is thrown sidearm with the intention of having it move in a line as the imaginary one that runs from the number two to the number eight on a clock, led to a relatively flat break. Rogers asked Yaccarino and his other pitchers to master the "Uncle Charlie" 12-6 curveball, which dives down akin to the line from the 12:00 to the 6:00 clock positions.[37] A well-thrown 12-6 curveball, if released at the correct height, appears to the batter as if it's headed above the strike zone, then dives into the heart of home plate. The same curveball released lower appears as if it's a good pitch to hit until it plunges to the batter's shoetops. (Ira Berkow, a prominent sports reporter, described a curveball of New York Mets' ace Dwight Gooden as "dropping as suddenly as a duck shot out of the air.")

"The 12-6 curveball," Rogers noted, "if thrown to the correct spots, is a devastating, unhittable pitch for Little League batters. It's close to impossible even for major leaguers to hit if someone like Koufax is throwing it." Rogers' reference was to Sandy Koufax, perhaps the greatest practitioner of the 12-6 curveball of all time.

In 1964, Koufax was in his prime and pitching for the Los Angeles Dodgers.[38] The story is told of Koufax facing Mickey Mantle in the opening game of the 1963 World Series between the Dodgers and the Yankees. (Koufax went 25–5 that year, leading Yogi Berra to quip, "I can see how he won twenty-five games. What I don't understand is how he lost five.") In the first inning, Koufax struck out Mantle, throwing only hummers. In Mantle's second at-bat, Koufax went up two strikes on him, again using only blazing fastballs. With Mantle anticipating another fastball, Koufax unleashed a curve that came in eye-level and then plunged, crossing the plate at Mantle's knees. Mantle flinched but never moved his bat. He stood frustrated in the batter's box as he was called out; then he turned to the catcher, Johnny Roseboro, and blurted out, "How the heck are you supposed to hit that crap?" (But Mantle said it more crudely.)

The 12-to-6 curveball thrown by a right-handed pitcher is especially effective against right-hand batters, which most

Little Leaguers are—a factor that would come into play in a significant way during tournament play.

To ensure that his pitchers mastered the 12-6 curveball, Rogers enlisted the help of Staten Island pitching legend Jack Hurley.[39] Hurley, born and raised in Westerleigh, had played in MILL. By 1964, he was a strapping right-hander with an exploding fastball and a standout at Port Richmond High School. The following year, he struck out 46 batters over a three-game playoff run to the New York City high school championship game. Hurley was so impressive in his senior high school year that upon arriving home after June graduation ceremonies, he and his family found local Yankees scout Al Cuccinello sitting on the front steps, contract in hand. Hurley ultimately turned down a hefty bonus offer from his favorite team to accept a scholarship to the University of Michigan.[40]

"Jack Hurley," Yaccarino recalled, "taught me how to throw a curveball with the correct follow-through so that when it came out of my hand, it was exactly at the twelve position, but by the time it reached home plate, it was at six. And he taught me how to toss it with control, which was key. I also learned to throw the curveball and fastball with the same motion, so the batter couldn't set himself up for either pitch."

By 1964, having a Little League pitcher throw any type of curveball was on the cusp of being taboo, blamed for arm injuries because it places torque on the elbow of a boy whose muscles and bones are not fully developed. Baseball great Carl Yastremski, who broke into the majors with the

Boston Red Sox in 1961, had been an outstanding pitcher on his Little League team on Long Island. But throwing too many curves hurt his arm to the point where, at times, he couldn't even pick up a baseball. Yastremski eventually gave up pitching, became an outfielder, and tormented American League hurlers for over two decades.[41]

Many fathers did not want to risk their son's arm by allowing him to throw a curve too early. "I was sensitive to that concern," Rogers admitted. "I'd constantly ask my pitchers how their arm felt. I didn't have them throw a lot of curves in practice. Only a few to make sure it was working. And the 12-to-6 curveball, which starts above the shoulder and is thrown like someone pulling down a shade, does not put maximum strain on the elbow, shoulder, or forearm."

One aspect of the game Rogers didn't teach was pitching philosophy, which involves matters such as setting up a batter to expect one type of pitch but then throwing another. Rather, he made clear that he would decide each pitch. Rogers believed that it was difficult for twelve-year-olds to both call pitches and execute them. "Also, that way, I'd be to blame if it was the wrong call." There were only a few basic variations in his repertoire—fastball in or out and up or down, or curveball in or out and up or down. Rogers would signal pitches to the catcher, with one finger for a fastball or two fingers for a curve, pointing up or down and with hand to thumb if inside or pulling on a string if outside. None of the pitchers ever thought to shake off Rogers' call. "Hell," Nugent quipped, "if I shook off a pitch, I probably would have been pulled out of the game."

Rogers charted on lined yellow paper every pitch thrown. "I knew what pitches each opposing batter saw during his first time at bat. So, for example, if my pitcher had started the batter off with a fastball the first time around, I'd likely call for a curveball to start off his second trip to the plate."

Rogers had his players practice multiple positions and skills to ensure his flexibility to mix and match should injuries, illness, and game situations require that. His pitchers were prime examples, particularly Paul, who in addition to being the number-two starter would play second base when Yaccarino pitched and move to third base when Nugent pitched. "Coach Rogers had a knack for utilizing our talents to the max," Paul remembered.

Rogers' roster included three excellent shortstops—Johnny Currado, Eddie Godnig, and Donny Quattrochi. Among them, Currado stood out. As depicted by Godnig, Currado "had a strong arm and was as swift as a rabbit with the hands of a saint. He was a natural field general." Joe Nugent, who has seen hundreds of Staten Island baseball games over the years, insists that Currado is the best shortstop to ever play on the Island.

Not surprisingly, Rogers decided that Currado would remain at shortstop, and shifted Godnig to right field. But he also wanted Quattrochi in the starting lineup for his hitting ability, strong arm, and quickness. He solved that problem, along with his most challenging positional dilemma, at the initial All-Star team practice. "None of those drafted," Rogers recollected, "had played behind home plate during the regular season. When the boys lined up to be told their fielding positions, I told Donny that there's equipment in the dugout and asked him to go look at it. He comes out a minute later and says to me, 'Mister Rogers, it's catcher's equipment. I'm not a catcher.' I responded, 'You are now.'"

The catching spot is vital to a sound defense and, arguably, the most complex position to master. As described by Miller Huggins, Hall of Fame baseball second baseman and manager who led the Yankees to their first World Series triumph in 1923, "A good catcher is the quarterback, the carburetor, the lead dog, the pulse taker, and the traffic cop...No team gets very far without one."

Rogers spent much time instructing Quattrochi on how to don and remove his catcher's gear (chest protector, shin guards, mask, and helmet) properly and swiftly. "It was even more difficult," Quattrochi recalled, "because the ones given me were too big."

Rogers stressed to Quattrochi the importance of preventing passed balls, which can abruptly change the tenor of the game. Each day, Rogers would have one of the fathers throw balls in the dirt in front of Quattrochi to have him become adept at blocking them. Other skills developed by Quattrochi through one-on-one instruction included foot and throwing arm positioning and how to alter his stance from relaxed to ready depending on whether there are runners on base, protect his throwing hand, release the ball quickly with a four-seam grip, and present the best throwing target with his mitt. Constant practice helped

Quattrochi overcome the natural fear that arises from a batter swinging a club over one's head.

Quattrochi became the glue of the entire defense, catching every inning of every tournament game near flawlessly. He developed his own version of baseball lingo that his teammates learned in order to understand his signals. He also kept the team loose with a wacky, lovable personality.

Quattrochi never played catcher after that 1964 All-Star season. "For the most part," he admitted, "I hated that position. Except for one thing, that you're involved in each pitch of the game."

In 1964, Little League did not yet have a mandatory play rule, so Rogers was able to establish a set defensive lineup, with Ebner at first, Paul at second, Currado at shortstop, Nugent at third, Quattrochi catching, Klee in center field, and Godnig in right field. This contributed to the team's consistent play. There were only two alterations. One was based on who pitched. Yaccarino would take the mound every other game. When Paul pitched, Yaccarino assumed his place at second. When Nugent pitched, Yaccarino played second, and Paul shifted to third.

The second disparity was a rotation among those who played left field, with Frank Higgins, Gary Kresge, and Richie Smiechowski each taking turns. "I didn't play in the first few tournament games," Smiechowski recounted. "But I practiced as hard as the starters, because Coach Rogers demanded that. And he expected the reserves to cheer the team on from the dugout and otherwise take part in the game."

The batting lineup also was fixed: Currado, Yaccarino, Paul, Ebner, Klee, Godnig, Quattrochi, Nugent, and whoever was playing left field.

By coincidence, the entire infield and battery, except for Currado, attended St. Rita's Elementary, the local Catholic parish's grammar school. "St. Rita's," Quattrochi recalled, "was another place where strict discipline was instilled in us. The teachers were mostly nuns who were no-nonsense types. And when you got in trouble in school, you got in trouble at home as well."

All the team members who attended St. Rita's knew each other well. "That further helped our cohesiveness," Paul noted. "We had played sports and hung out together for years before the 1964 tournament."

There was yet another advantage. As told by Yaccarino, "Before the game started, we would gather at the mound, crouch down, and collectively chant the Hail Mary prayer. I'm convinced that was the special ingredient that sealed the deal on our championship."

CHAPTER 9
Ruling the Big Apple

You could see on the faces of the guys on the other team how
intimidated they were. It always made me wish I had the
chance to play for Bill.

—Joe Nugent

IN 1964, MILL WAS seeking a third straight New York
City Little League championship, a feat that had never been
accomplished. Rogers was determined to make it happen,
which would require five wins in a row. To qualify for the
World Series in Williamsport would require an additional
five straight wins in state and regional tournament play.
A loss of any of those games, and MILL was out of the
tournament.

To prepare for the intensity of single-elimination play,
Rogers arranged for an exhibition game between his 1964
team (minus the eleven-year-olds on that team) and his 1963
team. "It was a great move by Bill," Jeff Paul opined. "We
knew them and looked up to them because they almost

made it to Williamsport. And they were a tough opponent being thirteen-year-old kids now playing Babe Ruth ball."

The game turned into a pitcher's duel won by the 1964 team 2–1. "Danny and Jeff pitched great," Johnny Currado recalled. "And we displayed a defensive performance that turned heads and ratcheted up our confidence." After the game, Rogers thought, "My 1964 team may not be as physically talented as the one from a year before, but it's more balanced and better defensively."

On July 25, 1964, MILL embarked on tournament play. Rogers wasn't looking past vying for the Staten Island championship, as he felt that his team's most difficult competition might be local. The first game, against the All-Stars of the East Shore Little League, was played in Weissglass Stadium in Mariners Harbor, a neighborhood that had been an oyster-industry hub during the 19th century. The stadium was named after Julius Weissglass, a stereotypical American immigrant success story. Weissglass, an Austrian Jew, emigrated to New York City in the late 1880s and found work in the famed Luchow's Restaurant in the East Village as a busboy and waiter. One day, he was sent to Staten Island to purchase horseradish from local farms. Weissglass fell in love with the countryside and bought a chicken farm, selling milk and eggs.

Decades later, he was a leading Staten Island philanthropist whose family ran a highly successful milk-processing and -bottling plant, one that Bobby Nugent's grandfather delivered milk for. "In those days," Nugent explained, "milk was delivered cold to front porches in glass bottles with collectible tops sealed with wax. After the milk was consumed, the bottles were washed, cleaned, and returned to the front porch to be replaced on a subsequent delivery."

As would become the routine, Rogers assembled the players an hour before the game. "We were required," Currado recalled, "to be dressed and ready to go with focus and attention to detail. I understood where the term "uniform" came from as each of us needed to be dressed the same way, with stirrup socks neatly tucked into our uniform pants. Hats were never allowed to be worn backwards."

Rogers was ahead of his time in applying professional baseball principles to Little League in a number of ways. One was reviewing with his team a brief report on the opponent's lineup, with critical help in that regard being provided by Mike Sosa. "My dad," recounted Eddie Sosa, one of Mike Sosa's seven sons, "after the tournament began, scouted every opposing team and kept a scorebook of each game. He would let Bill know, for each batter, things like whether he could hit a curveball, whether he could pull the ball, and where he liked the ball pitched. Similarly, my father gave Bill a rundown of the strengths of every pitcher he saw, including his velocity, types of pitches, control, and mannerisms."

Rogers, in turn, provided his players with Sosa's analysis of each hitter and of the starting pitcher. The other team's star performer was identified, with the phrase "Don't let this kid beat us" usually following. Afterward, the signs for the game were reviewed, with the keys for them being changed from game to game to prevent their theft. Rogers then discussed the ground rules of the field the game would be played on, as every field was different in terms of fences, backstops, and dead-ball areas.

No time went idle under Rogers' watch. When the opposing team was going through its drills, Rogers and the entire team observed, watching arm strength, accuracy, and how smoothly fielders were making plays.

Rogers taught the importance of beating the other team mentally and displaying a killer instinct. When it was MILL's turn for pre-game warmup, the team would huddle in front of the dugout. The players would let out a loud roar before sprinting full speed onto the field in a manner, as described by Currado, "similar to a synchronized swimming team all moving fluidly. Coach Rogers was adept at hitting fly balls that gave each fielder time to set up for a strong throw. Infielders received one-hop hard ground balls that seemed to bounce flawlessly into our gloves and allow us to set up for strong throws to first base and to second on double plays."

As Greg Klee explained, "There were no loose balls rolling around the infield or outfield being chased down. It was part of Bill's program to put the opponent on its heels before the first pitch was thrown. We ended our drill with each infielder fielding slow ground balls that were thrown to home plate. After the catcher received the throw, he rolled a ball to another charging infielder. As each infielder completed his drill, he waited on the first base foul line till the first baseman completed his toss to home plate." Joe

Nugent, who observed many of these pre-game routines, commented that "it looked like a precision military exercise."

MILL raced to a fast start in the opening inning when Klee singled with the bases loaded to drive in two runs. Then Eddie Godnig stepped to the plate with Klee and Billy Ebner on base. Cheering him on was Richie Smiechowski, coaching first base. (Only players were allowed to coach at first or third base.) Godnig and Smiechowski lived a few blocks away from each other and were close friends. "I was at Eddie's house all the time," Smiechowski recalled. "That's where I was introduced to Italian food." Smiechowski owed his MILL All-Star experience in part to Eddie's father, as his own father at the time was away serving as a Navy captain (one of three MILL Navy fathers). "One day that summer, as we often did, our family took an early-morning trip to the Brooklyn Navy Yard to see my dad off. Mom stayed at home with the four of us. She didn't drive, so Eddie's dad would give me lifts to and from practice."

Godnig waited on a fastball and blasted it to right field. Not certain how far he'd hit the ball, Godnig lowered his head and sprinted toward first base. Smiechowski watched as the ball cleared the fence and yelled, "'Eddie, slow down, it's a homer!'" Godnig was beyond thrilled. "I never thought," he admitted, "that I would begin my Little League tournament play with a home run. And against a pretty big pitcher who threw hard. Hitting the sweet part of a wooden bat with a ball ranks among the finest feelings humans can experience!"

The game was effectively over at that point, as Yaccarino was dominant, tossing a one-hitter. MILL drubbed East Shore, not a strong league at that time, 9–0. Following the game, Rogers gathered his team. "One down, twelve to go!" they chanted. The ritual of counting off the number of wins so far and how many to go to win the World Series would continue after every game.

Following two days of further intensive practice, Paul took the mound at Cascio Field and pitched a four-hit shutout against the Great Kills' National Division. He threw strikes consistently and used the 12-6 curve ball to have opposing batsmen fishing all game. MILL won 6–0, with Paul also contributing two hits.[42]

Even though Yaccarino was the star pitcher, several teammates considered Paul to be the team's MVP, owing to his versatility. In addition to excelling on the mound, Paul alternated at second base and third base. As described by Godnig, "Jeff was a terrific infielder. Fast and graceful as a gazelle and covering a lot of ground around second base. He sucked up anything near him. And he was the team's most consistent hitter, batting third because he rarely struck out and was adept at keeping an inning alive. Jeff always had a huge smile on his face and exuded self-assurance." In the spirit of baseball and nicknames having long been a congenial pair, Paul's agreeability led him to be given the moniker "Yup Yup."

The third tournament game, on August 1 at Buddy Cusack Field for the Staten Island Little League championship, was against the West Shore, MILL's greatest rival.

"Any game against West Shore was big," Ebner remembered. "Mid-Island and West Shore were right next to each other, and kids from each league played and went to school with each other."

West Shore's pitcher, Jim Gargulio, was rumored to have the best fastball on Staten Island. Another concern was that Gargulio was a lefty, as MILL's batters had little experience hitting against southpaws. "We didn't have lefty batting-practice pitchers," Yaccarino recalled. "Coach Rogers had to scrounge around to find a high school player who was lefty to throw to us."

Before five hundred fans, Yaccarino opened the game by walking the first batter he faced, who would come around to score. MILL promptly struck back. Currado, who led off the bottom of the first with a single, was the shortest member of the team. "I was very conscious of my height. I was usually in the front row in school pictures and wore the #1 uniform. In the summer of 1964, I was only 4'8" and 74 pounds. The offset was that I was the fastest and quickest player with enough power to drive the ball into the gaps."

Providing a small strike zone, and pound-for-pound with great offensive power, Currado was an ideal leadoff hitter. Rogers asked him to be a team leader as well, which the shortstop often is. "Coach Rogers," Currado explained, "trusted me to make sure that everyone in the infield always knew the game situation and was in the right place."

Currado was sacrificed to second by Yaccarino and advanced to third on a single by Paul. After Paul took second on a ground out by Ebner, Godnig singled in two runs.

Those were all Yaccarino needed as he struck out ten batters, allowing only three hits and leading MILL to a 3–1 victory. West Shore's lone run was the only one allowed by MILL in its initial three tournament games. MILL had advanced easily out of the tough Staten Island Little League district.

Next up was West Highway, the Brooklyn champs, in the semifinal of the New York City Little League playoffs. Rogers required each player to wear a shirt, tie, and sports jacket on the bus traveling to the Johnny DeRario Field in New Rochelle. Rogers told his team, "If you're gonna play good, you gotta look good, just like the Yankees do on and off the field."

Play "good" they did. Currado opened the top of the first with a line-drive double over the center fielder's head. After two were retired, Ebner, whose nickname was "Lil Abner," (the name derived from a long-running comic strip) stepped to the plate. Ebner was the biggest kid on the team, a muscular twelve-year-old at 5'10" and 180 pounds with excellent eye-hand coordination who could smash a baseball soundly and enjoyed a deserved reputation for timely hitting. In this at-bat, he lashed a double off the left center field wall, scoring Currado. MILL plated two more runners in the second with the benefit of wild pitches.

Paul returned to the mound and was even sharper than in his initial outing. His first inning was "immaculate" as he struck out the side on nine pitches. "I came off the mound, and I heard one of the West Side coaches say, 'Where did that curveball come from?'" Paul ended up pitching a two-hitter (one of those hits a homer in the second inning) while striking out nine and walking none. "That summer, when I pitched, I focused on always being around the plate. I didn't worry about getting hit hard because I had faith that one of the guys behind me was gonna catch the ball or make a great play on it."

The play of the day occurred in the bottom of the sixth when, with MILL ahead 3–1, Currado brought the fans to their feet when he fielded a grounder deep behind second base and fired a strike to Ebner to retire the batter by a step. Rogers howled with joy. "Johnny had terrific range," Rogers recalled, "including an ability to field balls on the other side of second base. Pitching and defense were what my 1964 team was known for. Most of the time, we didn't overpower teams like we had done the year before. The difference in 1964 was that we didn't give many runs away."

On August 6, the New York City title was up for grabs against a team from Glen Cove. (Glen Cove is located in Nassau County, outside of the New York City limits, but was allowed into the New York City tournament because there was no other league available to it then.) Glen Cove took an early lead in the top of the first inning when a "Baltimore chop" (a ball struck downward that bounces high in the air) allowed a runner to score from second when Quattrochi, backing up the throw to first base, left home plate unguarded.[43] The batter beat the throw to first from Yaccarino, and the runner on second base hustled around third and scored.

For years, Quattrochi and Yaccarino would tease each other about that play. "Danny would insist," Quattrochi explained, "that I should have stayed by home plate. My argument to him was that I was trained to back up first base on every ground ball, and that, after he threw to first, he should have run over to cover home plate. It's an argument that neither of us ever will win."

Yaccarino settled down and held Glen Cove scoreless the rest of the way, fanning ten and allowing only two bleeder singles. The Glen Cove batters never hit a fly to an outfielder. However, their pitcher, Mike Anander, likewise held MILL scoreless until there were two outs in the fifth inning. "We were four outs from elimination," Godnig remembered. "There was a lot of anxiety and tension surfacing in our body language." Yaccarino was frustrated. "The Glen Cove pitcher was good, but we helped him by hitting balls right at fielders." The dream appeared to be dying before it had commenced in earnest.

"One of the beautiful things about baseball," said all-time strikeout king Nolan Ryan, "is that every once in a while, you come into a situation where you want to, and where you have to, reach down and prove something." Currado had tears in his eyes as he stepped to home plate. But he and the rest of the MILL team were a fiercely competitive bunch and mentally strong. Rogers had taught them to "focus on the things you can control. As a batter, you don't control whether you get a hit or where exactly the ball will go. What you do control is your approach, thought process, and the type of swing you take."

Currado jumped on the first pitch, a high fastball, and smashed an opposite field blast that bounced off the top of the fence and over to tie the game. "Cascio Field had an eight-foot-high fence that I'd never cleared, even in practice. But this time, on this field, after I made contact, I looked up and thought, 'Whoa, this has a chance.'" When Currado returned to the bench, he realized that he'd mistakenly grabbed a bat that wasn't his usual 28-inch one but, rather, an inch longer and ounces heavier. "The extra weight helped me drive the ball over the fence without sacrificing bat speed. So, I thought, *Maybe I should have been using this bat all along.*"

It was one of the most memorable moments in Staten Island sports history. Joe Nugent, watching in the stands, was stunned. "We were losing to a good team and a very talented pitcher. It seemed like we were doomed. Then a kid who was under five feet and who had never homered in Little League competition crushes one." Bill Rogers shook his head in amazement. "That one at-bat turned the game around completely. And it gave Johnny a new nickname— "Mighty Mite." Greg Klee believes it was a moment of God's intervention. "Johnny never hit another home run that summer. It showed that we were blessed."

After Currado's homer, the Glen Cove starter was removed for another pitcher, which puzzled Rogers. "He was throwing well and had struck out a lot of our guys. I guess their manager was afraid his confidence had been shaken by being taken out of the park by such a little guy."

The game progressed into the bottom of the sixth, tied at 1–1. Paul lined a zinger off the shortstop's glove for a single and Ebner followed with a hummer past third, placing runners on first and second. Rogers sent Klee up with instructions to bunt. Klee missed the ball, but it bounced away from the catcher, allowing Paul and Ebner to move up a base. With the infield drawn in, Rogers gave Klee the green light. The new Glen Cove pitcher came in with a fastball. "It was a good pitch," Klee recounted, "and I only got the handle of the bat on it. The ball traveled maybe fifty feet, never leaving the infield. But with the first baseman drawn in, I got just enough lumber on the ball for it to bloop over his head." Before the second baseman could retrieve the ball and fire it home, Paul danced to the plate and jumped on it, handing MILL its third straight New York City Little League title.

CHAPTER 10
Intuition

Manager Bill (Nero) Rogers fiddled and Rome burned!
—*Staten Island Advance* (August 16, 1964)

TWO EVENTS OF American historical significance occurred during the first week of August 1964.[44] One was the start of the Vietnam War, which, over nine years, would kill more than 58,000 Americans and tear the nation apart. The other was the discovery of the bodies of civil rights workers James Chaney, Andrew Goodman, and Michael Schwerner in an earthen dam on a farm near Philadelphia, Mississippi, where they had disappeared weeks earlier. The murder of those men by members of the local White Knights of the Ku Klux Klan, with the active assistance of the Sheriff's Office and police, sparked national outrage and helped gain passage of the Civil Rights Act of 1964.

The MILL players remained in the throes of childhood bliss. "I never heard the adults talk about Vietnam or civil rights or any of the big news," Jeff Paul recalled. "I did have sisters who were obsessed with the Beatles and their new film *A Hard Day's Night*."

In the mid-afternoon of Saturday, August 8, a quarter-final game for the New York State championship took place in New Rochelle, with MILL facing off against the Kensico All-Stars from Valhalla, a hamlet in Westchester County. MILL trailed 1–0 after three innings. But in the top of the fourth, Paul tattooed a high fast ball over the left-center field wall to tie the score. The offensive floodgates burst wide open, with MILL plating eleven runs in the final two innings. A team that wasn't expected to hit with power smashed four homers, two by Billy Ebner. "The second one," Ebner reminisced, "was a looker. Went way over the fence. I felt like Mickey Mantle."

Meanwhile, Paul shut down Kensico, a club that had accumulated 25 runs and 27 hits in its last two games, hurling a six-hitter. Helping Paul out were the three ground ball double plays turned by the infield, two of which involved outs at third and second. "Currado, Nugent, and Yaccarino," Rogers observed, "played like mini-major-leaguers that day and throughout the tournament."

Double plays are devastating momentum killers, but turning one in Little League play is difficult because of the complex skills involved. The infielder receiving the flip or toss must arrive at the bag quickly while maintaining body control in order to be in the correct position to receive the ball, which must be timed well and thrown accurately to him. Then he has to release the ball as soon as possible while shifting his lead shoulder in the proper direction. The hands require precise positioning close to the body. And the infielder often needs to be able to hop up, simultaneously as the ball leaves his hand, to protect himself from the incoming baserunner.

Converting a double play in 1964 was even more impressive because that was in the "Wood Bat Era" (aluminum bats were not approved for Little League play until 1971), which allowed no room for error. An aluminum bat is lighter and can be swung more quickly. As a result, a ball hit with an aluminum bat comes at the fielder faster, providing more time for the necessary throws.[45]

MILL next traveled to the suburban community of Eastchester, New York, for a semifinal game against the All-Star team from New Hyde Park (a Long Island community), which took place on Thursday, August 13, on a picture-book field at the Concordia Collegiate Institute. Originally founded to train pastors for Lutheran congregations, Concordia was thirty beautiful acres fifteen miles north of New York City. Two thousand fans showed up, by far the biggest audience MILL had played in front of. "For the first time," Currado recalled, "I felt the need to make an effort to keep focused on the game and not be distracted by the emotions of the fans. And we all felt more pressure to perform at our highest level."

Babe Ruth once reputedly remarked, "It's hard to beat a person who never gives up." This game, perhaps more than any of their other twelve, was illustrative of MILL's resilience. New Hyde Park went ahead 2–0 in the bottom of the third when Yaccarino loaded the bases on two walks and a hit batsman and then, with two outs, gave up a double.

In the top of the fifth, five outs from elimination, Currado flied to center, but the fielder dropped the ball. After Yaccarino was nicked on the left arm, Ebner lined a single over shortstop, driving home Currado. A wild pitch brought home Yaccarino, who slid in headfirst to tie the game.

New Hyde Park came close to victory in the bottom of the sixth when, with two outs, Yaccarino gave up a single to the opposing pitcher, Ray Nawrocki, and then threw two wild pitches, allowing Nawrocki to reach third. Yaccarino, demonstrating great fortitude, struck out the opposing second baseman for the third out. "Each one of us," Ebner described, "felt we were gonna win. So we never panicked. That's part of what made that team so special." Rogers described himself as "always optimistic, but also nervous."

With the intensity level ever rising as outs were recorded, the seventh and eighth innings went scoreless. In the top of the ninth, with one out, Donny Quattrochi walked and took second on a wild pitch. After Frankie Higgins struck out, Bobby Nugent came to the plate. "I was uptight because this was the seventh tournament game, and I had yet to get a hit. I was something like oh-for-sixteen." Nugent came through with a line drive that skirted over the second baseman's glove. Quattrochi was given a green light at third and hook slid across home plate with the go-ahead run, helped by the right fielder fumbling the ball in his haste to throw home.

In those days, there was no pitch-count limit, allowing Yaccarino to continue pitching. (There was a limit on innings pitched, nine, and a prohibition on consecutive appearances.) He struck out the side in the bottom of the ninth. Overall, Yaccarino fanned fourteen and, for the second straight outing, allowed only two hits. "That was the game," Rogers recalled, "that convinced me this team was even better than my 1963 team."

In the next morning's *Staten Island Advance,* a newspaper widely read across the Island, there was a photo of Quattrochi's slide. Another picture showed fans cheering on the MILL team. "In one of those photos," Richie Smiechowski noted, "you can see my older brother Jack and his friend Sonny screaming and celebrating our win. It made that game even more meaningful to me."

The next day, no games were scheduled. Instead, it was planned that the four teams would travel to nearby Playland Amusement Park. But Coach Rogers wouldn't allow it for his squad. As with every off day, his boys were going to practice. "As three buses were pulling out," Rogers remembered, "they were waving and laughing at us. And I thought, *We'll see who's laughing tomorrow.*"

On Saturday, August 15, the finals of the New York State tournament had MILL taking on a team from Rome, a town in the middle of the state near the Adirondack Mountains. Two days earlier, in a game that also went nine innings, Rome had edged Corning 3–2.

Rogers intended to send Jeff Paul to the mound, but Paul had developed a problem. "Gripping the ball on the stiches, pitch after pitch, gave me a blister on the ring finger of my throwing hand." Rogers instead tabbed his regular third baseman, Bobby Nugent, as his starter for the first time in tournament play.

As did most parents, Nugent's mom and dad attended every tournament game. His mother, Irene, too nervous to watch the play, would pace beyond the fence, alternating between reciting the Holy Rosary and listening to the crowd while checking the score as best she could. Nugent's dad would sit by himself in the stands.

That day, as usual, Joe Nugent Senior was, along with his wife, the first to arrive at the field. As was his habit, he shook hands with each player coming off the bus. "When Bobby's dad asked me how I felt," Rogers recounted, "I replied, 'Wonderful! Because your son is pitching today.' Mr. Nugent's expression turned from smile to shock. I didn't see him until after the game. He joined his wife in walking behind the field from the left field foul pole to right field foul pole. I think that summer it was the parents who suffered the most emotional strain."

Nugent's start was inauspicious. "The first batter," he recalled, "nearly took my head off with a line drive up the middle." Rogers thought to himself, "What the hell did I do?" It turned out to be the sole hit Nugent allowed. He would become stronger as the game progressed, striking out nine, including the last six batters, and leading MILL to a 3–0 win. All three MILL runs were scored in the first inning without the benefit of a hit (they garnered only two the entire game) on poor fielding and mental lapses by the Rome team combined with stellar MILL bunting.

Bunting, as noted by Currado, who has watched or attended in person every Little League World Series since 1964, "is a highly effective tool in Little League. Any time a fielder in motion must make a play on the ball and throw to a base, bad things can happen for the defense." In the bottom of the first, Currado beat out a grounder to short. Yaccarino laid down a sacrifice bunt fielded by the Rome pitcher, whose errant throw struck Yaccarino on the back. With runners on first and second, Paul also bunted. The pitcher chose to throw to third, but too late to beat the speedy Currado to the bag. Bases loaded. After Ebner fanned, Klee grounded to the second baseman who threw wide to home plate, allowing Currado to score. Rome's defensive gaffes continued when Godnig hit a slow roller to shortstop. The fielder's throw to home plate was late, letting Yaccarino score. It was "déjà vu all over again" when Quattrochi grounded to the first baseman, who threw home late, allowing Paul to score. As told by Paul, "Coach Rogers saw an opportunity to frustrate and demoralize the other team, which wasn't strong enough defensively, and he took advantage of it. That put runs on the board early and kind of took them out of the game."

Seconds after Nugent struck out a Rome batter to end the game, he was carried off the field by his delirious team-mates. For the second year in a row, MILL gained the State title. Rogers held high hopes for qualifying for Williamsport, although this time his optimism was more guarded.

*

The Eastern Regional Tournament was held in Burnham Park in Morristown, New Jersey. MILL now was one of only four remaining teams from the 1,550 teams that began tournament play.

On Thursday, August 20, MILL's adversary was Smithfield, Rhode Island, which previously had beaten a talented Puerto Rican All-Star team. Smithfield's ace was Bobby Gargone, a six-foot-tall lefty with a reputation for throwing a blazing, difficult-to-connect-with fastball. But he didn't start, having rapped his head on the low dugout entrance prior to game time hard enough to be rushed to a nearby hospital for stitches. Facing Smithfield's number-two pitcher, Currado led off with a walk and was sacrificed to second by Yaccarino. Then Gargone appeared in the dugout and sprinted to the mound.

The discombobulated Gargone promptly walked Paul and hit Ebner, loading the bases. With Klee up, Gargone uncorked a wild pitch, allowing Currado to score. The southpaw ended up allowing seven additional runs, much of it attributable to lack of control as he gave up eight walks and six wild pitches on top of five hits. On the other hand, Yaccarino pitched another gem, mixing curves and fastballs and striking out eleven batters while allowing only four hits and two walks as MILL routed Smithfield 8–0. Later, Rogers would muse, "Gargone was quite a talent. If he hadn't gotten thrown off his game, that might have been a really tough six innings."

In the other semifinal, New London, Connecticut, defeated Connellsville, Pennsylvania, 3–1, due to a dominating performance by New London's starting pitcher, who struck out sixteen. Rogers was genuinely disappointed. "We were rooting for Connellsville because we wanted to eliminate them in 1964 like they had done to us in 1963."

Two days later, in front of 3,000 fans, MILL faced New London for the right to move on to Williamsport. Rogers selected Nugent instead of Paul to take the mound. Rogers' thinking was that while Paul had pitched quite effectively to date, he hadn't struck out as many batters as Rogers hoped for. "Any ball that's put into play," Rogers said, "is a potential problem, even with a great defense."

Paul believes there was another reason. "I never confirmed this with Bill," Paul admitted decades later, "but I think I know why he tabbed Bobby to start instead of me. I was fanatical about Little League and kind of an emotional wreck after every game. So much so that I would cry with happiness after I pitched and won. And Coach Rogers would look at me with concern and ask, 'You okay, Jeff?' I think he became worried that I might unravel on the mound. In any event, it turned out to be a good call by him."

Rogers also, for the first time, started Richie Smiechowski in left field. "Coach Rogers came up to me before the game," Smiechowski recollected, "'out of left field' so to speak, and told me I was playing. I was euphoric, having the chance to roll with the big guns. And young enough not to overthink the pressure involved." Rogers later explained, "Richie wasn't as good a hitter as Gary

Kresge or Frank Higgins, the other two guys who platooned in left field. But he was the fastest left fielder and the best one defensively, and I was a defensive coach."

Albert Einstein once observed, "The only real valuable thing is intuition." Rogers' gut feeling proved to be spot on. With MILL ahead 1–0 in the top of the third, Nugent loaded the bases with one out. "I threw a fastball to their cleanup batter," Nugent recalled, "that wasn't fast enough. He slammed a shot down the left field line. Amazingly, Shmo [Smiechowski's nickname] tracked it down and made a backhand catch inches above the ground. It was the pivotal play of the game. If the ball had fallen and gotten behind him, we likely would have been down two runs with a runner at second or third. It would have been demoralizing. Instead, they were the ones demoralized."

After Smiechowski's catch quelled New London's rally, MILL exploded in the fourth and fifth innings for twelve runs on sixteen hits. Ebner went four-for-four (six for seven in the two Eastern Regional games) and Quattrochi three-for-four. Rogers was given the opportunity to insert all the subs. Meanwhile, Nugent settled down and pitched another strong game, yielding only three hits, with New London's lone run scoring on a wild pitch. The defense again was outstanding.

The weeks of practice, focus, and passionate commitment of fourteen boys, two coaches, and dozens of parents had paid off. Against the odds, the extraordinary occurred. MILL was on its way to the Little League World Series.

CHAPTER 11
The Promised Land

Each of the other seven teams was the enemy. We were there to win the World Series, not to fraternize.

—Johnny Currado

BASEBALL IS EMBEDDED in American consciousness. And no towns are more associated with the sport's remembrance and tradition than two pastoral ones, Williamsport, Pennsylvania, and Cooperstown, New York, home of the Baseball Hall of Fame.

Williamsport, nestled in a valley within mountains lush with pine-tree forests, lies on the banks of the Susquehanna River. That river provides a geographic link between Williamsport and Cooperstown, as its north branch begins 200 miles away as the outlet of Otsego Lake, which Cooperstown borders on the south. In an eerie coincidence, the Hall of Fame opened its doors on June 12, 1939, only six days after the first Little League game was played. Yet another connection between the two towns is that each swells with life in the summer due to a baseball event. For Cooperstown, the draw is Hall of Fame Weekend at the end of July, while Williamsport hosts the Little League World Series a month later.

Incorporated in 1823, Williamsport was formed as a market stop for the benefit of local farms. In 1847, the first "log boom" was established on the river at a relatively flat point near the town, an ideal location for a series of piers with heavy chains strung between them used to entrap logs as they floated down river. Over the ensuing decades, cutters sent millions of logs of white pine, Eastern hemlock, and other hardwoods from the Allegheny Mountains down the Susquehanna to Williamsport's sawmills.

Williamsport became the lumber capital of the nation, where "Lumber Barons" earned their fortunes. (After the Civil War, Williamsport boasted of having more millionaires than any other American town.) Those moguls helped create an elegant downtown with spectacular Victorian homes, the vestiges of which are located on West 4th Street, known as "Millionaires Row." This prosperity was short-lived, as floods during the late years of the 19th century swept away much of the town, and lumber-processing plants sprung up in other locales. By the early 20th century, most of the eastern U.S. was devoid of old-growth forest as a result of careless logging practices. Williamsport's claim to fame turned from lumber to Little League baseball.

Rogers had told his kids before tournament play began, as a motivational device, that if they qualified for Williamsport, they would travel there by plane. The boys, none of whom had ever flown, were pumped up about that prospect. But the promise went unrealized due to the league's budgetary limits.

Instead, the MILL team's drive from Morristown to "the Show" was a bumpy ride on a non-air-conditioned bus during a sultry day. As there was no interstate then, with Route 80 being a single hilly lane in each direction, the trip took five hours. Making matters worse was that Frankie Higgins, one of the reserves, became "bus sick." "We were jumping out of our skins in excitement to get there," Greg Klee recalled, "but had to keep stopping for Frankie to get out and throw up. At one point, the driver let him sit on the floor by the top step of the bus to expedite the process."

The boys made the best of the situation. "The Four Seasons were really popular then," Jeff Paul reminisced. "We entertained ourselves by busting chops and singing songs like 'Sherry' and 'Walk Like a Man' in doo-wop style."

Any lingering aggravation was forgotten when the bus arrived in South Williamsport and pulled off of winding Route 15 at a high spot with a view of Lamade Stadium directly below. Whooping and hollering, the MILL boys dashed off the bus and gazed down at their field of dreams, perfectly manicured with deep, golden-brown dirt and bright, finely cut Kentucky bluegrass that appeared as a woven green rug. "I was as awestruck," Eddie Godnig recalled, "as when I went to Yankee Stadium for the first time. The first- and third-base boundaries were straight as an arrow, and the outfield fence, bases, and mound were pure white. It was breathtaking, one of the few occasions when reality exceeded expectations." For Greg Klee, "it was like seeing the promised land after forty years in the desert. Cascio was a pretty nice field, but this was way beyond nice."

A Little League host, Peter Lupecchino, who the boys called "Uncle Pete," was waiting for the team in the fenced-in players village compound. He led them to the cabin, modest and largely unfurnished except for bunk beds, in which they would stay for the week. "We were separated from our parents," Bobby Nugent recalled, "which was a big deal at that age."

The boys quickly took note of the Olympic-sized swimming pool on premises. "It was hot," Donny Quattrochi explained, "and the pool was gorgeous, but we knew Coach Rogers wouldn't let us swim because he believed it took too much strength out of us."

Each boy was weighed and measured. "I remember," Nugent observed, "that I was 5'2" then, because by the next summer, when I played Babe Ruth baseball, I had grown to 5'10". The team was provided with schedules and issued practice and game wool uniforms with "EAST" boldly displayed on the front.

An enduring trait of baseball players at all levels is the adherence to superstitions of varying levels of rationality, such as not changing underwear during a winning streak, talking to the baseball, or tapping your shoes before assuming a batting stance. One of MILL's superstitions was that they must eat pizza prior to each game. Even though Little League provided free meals, the team ordered in pizza every night they were in Williamsport. "I probably ate more pizza that summer," Klee admitted, "than in the next five years of my life."

*

From its inaugural 1947 tournament through 1956, the World Series was composed predominantly of U.S.-based teams. (One Canadian team played in 1952 and another in 1953.) By 1964, however, the eight teams in the tournament represented four domestic regions (Central, East, South, West) and four international ones (Canada, Europe, Far East, Latin America).[46] There was a single bracket, with the quarter-final matchups drawn randomly. The tournament remained single elimination, heightening the tension.[47]

That summer, the U.S. champion teams in addition to MILL were La Puente, California (in a suburb of Los Angeles), Mobile, Alabama, and Bartlesville, Oklahoma (the last team coached by one-time Oklahoma University All-America basketball guard Ken Pryor).[48] On the international side, the Canadian team for the second straight year was from Valleyfield, Quebec, the European team from Wiesbaden, Germany, the Far East team from Tachikawa City, Japan, and the Latin American team for the fifth straight year from Monterrey, Mexico. Key to allowing the "World" in "World Series" to have meaning was the support of Pan Am Airlines. Pan Am's assistance was enlisted after the 1959 World Series when the European champion team from the Bad Kissingen Airfield in Bavaria was prevented from competing because flight arrangements could not be completed in time. Pan Am transported European and Japanese teams on Jet Clippers leaving from Frankfurt and Tokyo, respectively, and even provided guides for the boys and their coaches to ease the passage.

The international nature of the Little League World Series enriched it and heightened its popularity. But it also presented challenges. One regarded reviewing birth certificates to ensure that all players were not older than twelve as of August 1 of the current year. Although routine, there was not the intensity to the process that would arise decades later after two scandals erupted. In 1992, Zamboanga City, a Philippines team, won the World Series but then was determined to have brought to Williamsport a squad entirely comprised of players either past the age cutoff (who used the identities of younger children) or who were shipped in from outside the zone of eligible residence.[49] In 2001, another Danny—Danny Almonte, born in the Dominican Republic—was pitching for the Rolando Paulino All-Stars of the Bronx. His 75-mph fastball (the equivalent for the shorter Little League mound-to-plate distance of a 100-mph major-league fastball) made him near unhittable. He tossed a perfect game in World Series competition, but later was found to have been fourteen years old that summer.[50]

In 1964, a more innocent, unsophisticated time as these matters go, the Williamsport officials had difficulty understanding the Japanese birth certificates, because the traditional Japanese calendar is used for official documents. That calendar is based on the reign period of the emperor. Each time a different emperor begins his rule, a fresh counting of the years commences, and the period acquires a new name. The Tachikawa City players all were required to be born in either 1951 or 1952, which were the 26th and 27th years of the "Shōwa" era (the reign of Emperor Hirohito). It took a while for the officials to sort out that methodology.

*

For meals, each of the eight teams trooped to a large cafeteria where they ate communally, facilitating social interactions. "I was constantly explaining to others, including Americans, where Staten Island was," Klee remembered. Exchanges with the Japanese and Mexican boys were challenging as they spoke limited English. Further bonding opportunity was provided by the game room, containing ping pong and pool tables. "The Japanese players were really good at ping pong," Godnig recalled. "Which made me think they'd be good at baseball." Klee found the Japanese to have an intense interest in American items. "I made friends by handing out extra bubble gum."

Each meal was preceded by the ringing of an outdoor bell. "Once the bell sounded, every team was supposed to line up outside their cabin and head for the cafeteria," Currado explained. "The Japanese kids were very disciplined. They'd immediately rush out and stand at attention. The first morning, at about 10:30, Donny and I snuck out and rang the bell. The Japanese kids and their coaches ran out quickly and lined up, and then looked around confused about what they were supposed to do next. We did that the following morning as well and then stopped, figuring we'd get caught."

The MILL boys were struck by the international players' displays of cultural identity. The Mexicans wore vaquero dress, highlighted by sombreros, their first time entering the cafeteria. The Japanese stood and prayed before each meal. "One time," Nugent said with a chuckle, "while we were saying grace, the Japanese players sang to the tune of 'I've Been Working on the Railroad.' We all cracked up."

"Looking back," Smiechowski said, "I wish I'd taken more advantage of our proximity to the foreign players. But Bill made us focus on baseball, so we pretty much stayed to ourselves. We knew we had a job to do."

CHAPTER 12
You Ready, Eddie?

How could a New York City newspaper put California in the
headlines instead of their native sons?

—Eddie Godnig

PRIOR TO THE START of the World Series, a New York
Daily News sports section article declared that La Puente
was the favorite, perhaps a lazy call pinned on the fact that
a team from California had won the three previous Little
League World Series championships. "That pissed us off
and motivated us," Eddie Godnig recalled. Rogers was
unperturbed. "No one paid much attention to us. No one
gave us much of a chance. Which was better. Less pressure."

La Puente suffered a key loss before play began when its
star player, center fielder Randy Walls, collided with right
fielder David Weeks while chasing a fly ball, fracturing his
left arm. In the hospital, Walls was afforded the option to
be given a sedative while his arm was immobilized in a
cast and remain resting in bed or have it mended without

anesthesia and rejoin the tournament as a cheerleader on the bench. He chose the latter and never whimpered during the procedure. Later, his cast was autographed by the entire Japanese and Mexican teams.

On Tuesday, August 25, the first day of World Series play, La Puente was upset in the quarterfinal-round by Mobile.[51] In the earlier game played that day, Monterrey, Mexico, playing with borrowed equipment from local players because their own had been lost in travel to Williamsport, whipped Bartlesville 7–2. Monterrey scored all of its seven runs in the third inning when the Bartlesville defense fell apart.

The next day, Wednesday, August 26, 1964, MILL took the field against players from Wiesbaden, a city in central Germany near Frankfurt renowned for its thermal springs The Wiesbaden team had enjoyed a smooth flight to the U.S. but then its bus from the local airport, six miles away, broke down and the squad was pressed into duty, having to push the vehicle to the side of the road.

The game began at two p.m. as the first of a doubleheader. Thousands of fans jammed the bleachers as well as the two grassy semicircle ledges beyond the outfield fence located on the famous undulating hill (known as "the Hill" by all). There, they waited on lawn chairs and blankets with coolers as they picnicked, killing time by throwing baseballs and Frisbees and sliding down the Hill on makeshift cardboard sleds.

An hour before start time, the MILL team ran onto the field for drills. Tossing batting practice once again was Phil

Ebner. "My dad," Billy Ebner recalled, "was not an official coach, so he wasn't allowed to stay with the team. But he was always there for us."

MILL's opponent was "European" merely in a technical sense as the players were the sons of American soldiers based at Germany's Clay Kaserne, the headquarters of the U.S. Army's European operation. That the team from Germany was composed of Americans was not surprising, as baseball was a niche sport at best in that country. The first official baseball game in Germany was played at the 1936 Berlin Olympics, when baseball was a demonstration sport, but the only two teams that competed were from the United States.[52]

After World War II, baseball was popularized by American soldiers stationed in Germany, in line with the U.S. military's longstanding tradition of spreading interest in the game, which began during the Civil War. At that war's start, baseball largely was a regional sport centered around New York. By its end, baseball had been played by tens of thousands of Northern and Southern troops across the country and was on its way to becoming the national pastime. The first professional baseball teams soon followed, beginning with the Cincinnati Red Stockings in 1869.

Carl Stotz paved the way for the creation of European Little Leagues in 1955 when, at the invitation of the U.S. Defense Department, he and Johnny Lindemuth, executive secretary of Little League, embarked on a tour of American military bases throughout Europe. Their first stop was at Garmisch-Partenkirchen, a Bavarian ski resort in Germany near the Austrian border, converted to military use. Stotz and Lindemuth were hosted by legendary General Anthony McAuliffe, then commanding general of the Seventh Army.[53] Stotz sold McAuliffe and the Army on the benefits of introducing Little League to servicemen's sons.

MILL had gotten lucky having been randomly chosen by draw to play Wiesbaden in the quarterfinal round, as that team was reputed to be the weakest of the eight, understandable in view of its limited pool of participants. Over the decades, European teams largely have not been competitive at the highest levels of Little League. No team from the European region has ever reached the finals of the World Series.

Rogers weighed whether to start Danny Yaccarino or preserve him for stronger competition. Yaccarino had come down with a 24-hour-flu when the team arrived in Williamsport and spent the night in the Little League complex's infirmary, dosed with antibiotics. He was released the next morning, but still in a weakened state.

Also wanting to save Paul and Nugent for the later games, Rogers warned Eddie Godnig that he might take the mound. Godnig, who had pitched during the regular season but not at all during All-Star competition, felt butterflies. "To calm myself, I thought about all the practice pitching games I'd played with my dad."

Before the game, Rogers chose Yaccarino to start. Rogers won the coin toss to determine which would be the home team and, as usual, chose to bat second. When the MILL players took the field, they were greeted with roars from the crowd, which included twelve busloads of friends and family members.

After a 1-2-3 top of the first, MILL jumped ahead in the bottom of the inning, scoring six runs aided by six walks and a throwing error by pitcher Hans (Butch) Quigley, a West Berlin native adopted by a U.S. Army sergeant. Twelve players batted in the first inning, in which two hits, three walks, two errors and three wild pitches produced six runs. The only substantial blow was a two-run double by Godnig. "Quigley," Godnig recalled, "was around six feet, but fortunately not as good as his height suggested." (Long limbs are beneficial for pitchers, who can turn that extra distance between the shoulder and the hand into fastball velocity.)

Regarding MILL's first inning, a *New York Times* sports reporter would write, "For a while, it seemed as if the score might mount into the hundreds." Over six innings, Quigley gave up seven walks and three wild pitches, allowing MILL to score eight runs overall on only four hits.

In contrast, Yaccarino retired the first nine Wiesbaden batters in a row. In the middle of the third inning, Rogers motioned Yaccarino over to his side of the bench and told him, "I'm sure you could pitch a no-hitter, but let's save your strength. You okay if I pull you?" "Sure, Mr. Rogers" was the response. Rogers inserted Godnig. Years later, Rogers admitted to Yaccarino that he would have taken him out of the game no matter what his answer had been.

It didn't begin well for Godnig, who immediately walked two batters and then balked them over a base. Balks are common among Little League pitchers, who are prone to becoming anxious and moving out of the set position prematurely. Rogers strode to the mound. "I was thinking about giving Eddie the hook. Instead, I just told him to start throwing strikes." To Godnig's credit, he settled down and, with the help of solid defense, escaped without giving up a run that inning. Godnig and Yaccarino combined on a one-hitter as MILL crushed Wiesbaden 8–1.

After the game, the MILL players climbed into the wood and steel stands and watched as Tachikawa City defeated Valleyfield in a nail-biter that went scoreless until the bottom of the sixth, when the Canadian pitcher walked in the only run of the game. Few in Williamsport that August were aware of the significance of Tachikawa City, located in the western part of the Tokyo metropolis. During the late 1930s and throughout World War II, it was the site of an airfield, an Air Academy, and critical aircraft manufacturing facilities all operated by the Imperial Japanese Army. In the closing months of the war, Tachikawa was bombed day and night by squadrons of B-29s. After the war ended, the base was rebuilt and placed back into operation as the main troop carrier base of the Far East Air Forces.

Rogers and his players were impressed by the Tachikawa City squad, who demonstrated what the Japanese term "*konjo*," a prized value that refers to the will and tenacity to persevere. "They were scrappy, skilled, knew what to do on offense and defense, made no mistakes, and hustled all the time," Smiechowski remembered. "They seemed very tough mentally." Rogers understood that Tachikawa City had practiced and prepared rigorously in a manner similar to his methods. "But if they also were a machine," he assured himself, "we were an even bigger and harder one."

CHAPTER 13
No Lefties

I was watching the Japanese third-base coach give signs by touching his hat and rubbing his arm. And I thought, why doesn't he just yell in Japanese? None of us would know.

—Bobby Nugent

BASEBALL HAS DEEP ROOTS in the "The Land of the Rising Sun," as much a part of that nation's culture as it is in America although more focused on the amateur game. The sport has linked two nations with vastly divergent histories and societies for a century and a half. At the 1964 Summer Olympics held in Tokyo, baseball again was a demonstration sport. 50,000 fans watched the sole game in which a U.S. team of college baseball players, including eight future major leaguers, defeated a Japanese amateur all-star team 6–2.[54]

Baseball was introduced in Japan in 1872 as a school sport by American Horace Wilson, a Civil War veteran who was an English professor at the Kaisei Academy in Tokyo.

It quickly flourished, but with a Japanese bent—viewed as a means of forging moral character. In the early 20th century, visiting Japanese warships fielded teams that played against American ones, and Japanese and American college baseball teams competed in goodwill tours. Most notably, in 1934, though the clouds of war were looming, an American all-star team led by Babe Ruth and including Jimmie Foxx, Lou Gehrig, and Charlie Gehringer barnstormed through Japan on a month-long, eighteen-game tour playing before hundreds of thousands of spectators. (Also on the U.S. team was Moe Berg, a journeyman catcher who was a spy secretly shooting films of Tokyo that were used by the Allies during World War II.) Swatting thirteen four-baggers, waving American and Japanese flags, clowning with kids, and even donning a kimono, the Babe was dazzlingly popular with the Japanese fans. Two years after that tour, the first professional Japanese baseball league was formed.

During World War II, Japanese soldiers taunted U.S. troops during several Pacific Island battles by screaming, "To hell with Babe Ruth!" Japanese-Americans interned in camps in the United States during the war used baseball to pass the time. Legend has it that five-star general Douglas MacArthur, who played baseball in high school and as a cadet at West Point, exploited baseball tactics during World War II to inform his military strategy—often quoting the well-known saying of Hall of Fame right fielder Wee Willie Keeler, "Hit 'em where they ain't."[55] MacArthur, while overseeing the occupation of Japan, used the sport as a means of promoting goodwill.

A Japanese team first participated in the Little League World Series in 1962. Less than twenty years after the end of World War II, the Japanese team was a crowd favorite. Their players, who could only say "hello," "goodbye," and "no English," used sign language to communicate. One of them, Tomio Takashima, became friends with Jim Hilsher of Montoursville, a village a few miles from Williamsport, after the two walked together around the sprawling complex. Before he returned to Japan, Takashima gifted Hilsher a pin he had brought from Japan and taught him jiujitsu tricks. Two weeks later, they inaugurated a simple correspondence that lasted for decades.

The difference in cultures—American individualism and free spirit versus the Japanese emphasis on harmony, formality, and conformity—was stark. On the bus from the local airport to the Little League complex, the Tachikawa City team played small wind instruments and sang the Japanese version of the nursery rhyme "Clap Your Hands." On game days, the Japanese marched into the stadium in perfect unison, each boy dressed in blue over-blouses. Before the beginning of each inning, the team gave a cheer led by the catcher, who would stand in front of the plate and yell in Japanese "Are you ready?" The other eight would scream back, "We are ready! Let's go!" And each of their batters would bow to the umpire prior to taking his stance.

Before the game, each team was allowed a half hour for infield and outfield practice on the main field. Tachikawa City went first. "They put on a good show," Johnny Currado remembered. "But then we went out and wowed the fans, with Coach Rogers doing his usual, using a fungo bat to hit vicious ground balls on one hop to each infielder that we handled cleanly. After we finished, the Japanese kids came out of the dugout, took their hats off, and bowed to us."

MILL, the visiting team for this game, failed to score in the top of the first against Tachikawa City's pitcher, Nagatoshi Shimizu. Bobby Nugent, tabbed by Rogers to start, had his concerns. "The Japanese kids were the shortest we ever faced, so I was forced to pitch to a shrunken strike zone. Fortunately, my control that day was good, as it usually was. What really worried me was that the Canadian pitcher threw harder than I could, and the Japanese kids hit his fastball. But Coach Rogers had me throw mostly curveballs, and it was clear that those guys had never faced a good curveball pitcher."

Japan's cultural norms led to the Tachikawa City players' highly skilled and meticulous approach. But they were disadvantaged in one vital aspect—Japanese children are brought up to be righthanded. One reason is that writing Japanese with the left hand is more difficult. Also, it's considered bad manners to use chopsticks in the left hand. The Tachikawa City manager, Yasuo Monoi, the principal of a kindergarten, told a reporter, "If I had a son, I wouldn't allow him to be lefthanded." Left-handed batters have an advantage against a right-handed pitcher such as Nugent. But there were no left-handed batters in the Tachikawa City lineup.

Nugent set the Tachikawa City team down in order in the first. That it was Nugent's day to shine became apparent in the top of the second, when he drove in the game's first two runs with a single to right. Jeff Paul added an RBI in the next inning. Meanwhile, Tachikawa City didn't develop a strong chance to score against Nugent until the fifth inning, when their best hitter walked to the plate with two on and two outs. After a couple of foul balls on curves, a fastball outside, and curve outside, Rogers approached the mound. "I told Bobby to throw a fastball inside on his hands. And that's what he did. The batter was expecting a curve and didn't move. He just looked at it, and we got the call. I slammed the dugout bench so hard I thought I broke my hand. I knew we had the game won because their Mr. Everything was out of the way."

With two out in the bottom of the sixth, the game ended on a steal play. Stealing typically is not an active offensive strategy in Little League baseball as no leads are allowed for runners and a runner cannot leave his base until after the ball passes the batter. But the Japanese team played aggressively and favored delayed steals.

"Bobby threw ball four to the batter," Donny Quattrochi recalled. "There was a runner on second who left for third on a delay. I threw the ball before realizing that Jeff wasn't covering the bag. The ball flew into left field and the runner scored. The batter rounded first and tried to take second. Fortunately, Richie hustled over, grabbed the ball, and threw it to Johnny who was covering second and smoothly tagged the kid out."

MILL was one win away from achieving the dream.[56] Their obstacle was the Obispado Little League All-Star team from Monterrey, Mexico. Obispado, which in the first game of the doubleheader that day edged Mobile, Alabama 4–3, would be chasing an unprecedented third title for its hometown. It had scored eleven runs in its two wins in Williamsport. And Monterrey's star pitcher, Julian Castillo, set to start in the championship game, was reputed to be near unhittable.

In two days, a bunch of American boys whose life experiences were limited by their age and modest backgrounds would face off against the Little League's equivalent of the New York Yankees. And they would do so under the glare of an international spotlight. Six innings of glory or heartbreak. Six innings that would define, in part, their entire lives.

CHAPTER 14
Autograph Time

*I would have liked to have had them [the MILL infield] in
St. Louis when I owned the Browns.*

—Bill Veeck

Similar to Japan, Mexico has a rich baseball tradition. The
sport has been played there since the late 19th century and is
second in popularity only to soccer in much of the country.
During the first half of the 20th century, Mexican baseball
fields became a safe haven for African-American teams
facing rampant discrimination in the U.S. The Mexican
Baseball League, in existence since 1925, has produced
dozens of major leaguers, with perhaps the best known
one being the pitcher Fernando "El Toro" Valenzuela. Ted
Williams, arguably the greatest hitter in baseball history,
who played from 1939 to 1960, was of Mexican-American
heritage, but hid that fact in order to avoid facing prejudice
from fellow players and fans.

In 1957, the Little League World Series was opened to teams outside the U.S. and Canada and crowned its first non-U.S. champion, from Mexico's Monterrey Industrial league. Monterrey, the capital and largest city of the state of Nuevo León, is the commercial center of northern Mexico and the base for many large Mexican and international corporations. That team was composed of boys who grew up in the Cantú neighborhood, a shantytown for families whose fathers and sons labored in the city's factories. They had started with baseball a few years earlier by clearing a debris-filled dirt field upon which they played barefoot with a homemade ball and gloves.[57]

Monterrey's opponent in the final game was from Northern La Mesa, California, whose players on average were significantly taller and heavier. The starting pitcher for the Mexican team was Angel Macias, known as "El Flaco" (the "Thin One"), a natural righty who taught himself to also pitch lefty after learning that his idol Sandy Koufax, then with the Brooklyn Dodgers, was a lefty. (Upon hearing that Koufax was Jewish, Angel announced that he, too, was "Joo-weesh.") Throwing right-handed, Macias was dominant, with eleven strikeouts, no walks, and not a single batted ball leaving the infield or runner reaching first as Monterrey won 4–0. His perfect game remains the only one tossed in Little League World Series finals history.[58]

By 1964, Monterrey was a Little League World Series powerhouse, with teams from that city having appeared in the four previous World Series and in seven overall. Their return to the championship game was heralded throughout

Mexico. Its team was now widely favored to gain their third title, one reason being that, in contrast to the situation in 1957, the Mexican players on average were taller and heavier than their American counterparts. "We joked," Danny Yaccarino recalled, "that they must have forgotten their birth certificates, because it looked like some of them were shaving."

MILL appeared jinxed. On Friday, August 28, the day before the final game, during a 90-minute morning practice, Yaccarino was stung on the pitching hand by a bee. Coach Klee accompanied him up the steep Hill to a Red Cross facility. While Yaccarino was being attended to, Klee collapsed onto a chair struggling to breathe. He was rushed to the hospital with what was feared to be a heart attack. It turned out that Klee had suffered an attack of angina, and he was released after a few hours. "Us kids weren't informed," Greg Klee noted. "Which was a good thing, particularly for me. I think my dad had reacted to all the stress, pressure, and hours."

Yaccarino, who Donny Quattrochi referred to as "Mr. Hollywood," was unperturbed by his swollen finger, announcing to anyone who would listen, "We're gonna be world champions."

After the practice, the MILL boys traipsed back to their cabin and showered. "We were just sitting around bored," Jeff Paul recalled. "Coach Rogers gave Bob Klee and Mike Sosa strict instruction to not allow us to exert ourselves in any way so we couldn't get injured or overtired. But then Rogers had to leave to attend a Little League meeting at their headquarters building. As soon as he left, Klee and Sosa bought souvenir bats and balls we'd been given. They split us up, and we went out and played. As we were finishing up, Rogers comes walking back and spots us. He starts yelling, 'What the hell is going on!'"

That evening, Yaccarino decided to sneak out of the cabin. He cajoled a reluctant Quattrochi to accompany him. The two hopped a fence and sat on top of the Hill, gazing down on the idyllic karma while Yaccarino repeated his brash prediction. Reflecting back, Quattrochi said, "I've always wondered how Danny and I were able to slip out and return without being caught. My guess is that Coach Rogers, together with Bobby Klee, Mike Sosa, and Phil Ebner, were down at the local gin mill tossing back a few."

The next day, August 29, dawned sunny and warm, with the temperature stretching into the 80s by the afternoon. In the morning, a Little League administrator entered the MILL cabin to reinforce certain rules, including no cursing, no throwing bats, and, of course, no fighting. "He also told us," Paul recounted, "not to touch ourselves, which I thought was pretty funny. When he left, we huddled around Coach Rogers, who asked us to focus on what we had to do, in spite of the hordes and the TV cameras."

As thunderclouds skirted Lamade Field, the consolation game began at 10 a.m. In a thriller, Mobile edged Tachikawa City 3–2.

Before their game, as if they were professionals at the major's World Series, the MILL twelve-year-olds were pounced upon by fans who persistently pressed onto them hats, programs, baseballs, and other items to sign. "It was so weird," Bobby Nugent recalled, "being asked for an autograph by older kids and adults. If I had known, I would have worked on perfecting my handwriting." The press box was filled with local and out-of-town newsmen. Various photographers wandered the field requesting poses, including one from Rogers' employer, Procter & Gamble.

ABC TV personality Sonny Fox, witty and congenial, who at the time hosted a long-standing TV show for kids called *Wonderama*, interviewed Yaccarino, who told Fox, "Boy, that infield of ours, it's nice to have them behind you."[59]

Fox then interviewed Nugent, who guaranteed victory in a tone reminiscent of the brash, charismatic Muhammad Ali. (Ali, before his February 1964 bout with then reigning heavyweight champ, Sonny Liston, assured the world that he'd win, which he did.) When needled by his teammates for having possibly jinxed them, Nugent refused to back down. "No way we're going to lose," he defiantly responded. "I truly believed," Nugent later explained, "that no one would hit Danny. It was just a matter of us getting some runs."

Per his standard ritual, Rogers reviewed with his players the strengths and weaknesses of the opponent's lineup and starting pitcher. As usual, the information largely was provided to Rogers by his undercover agent, Mike Sosa, of Puerto Rican origin, who spoke fluent Spanish. During Monterrey's prior two games in Williamsport, Sosa sat in the stands near the Monterrey dugout, watched and listened carefully, and took notes.

The gregarious Sosa became friendly with the Obispado Little League president. That connection quickly came in handy when Sosa realized that he lacked tickets for himself and his son for the championship game. Sosa asked for two tickets from a MILL official but was blown off, as tickets on the MILL side were in high demand and Sosa wasn't a family member of a player. Sosa then went to the Obispado Little League president, who promptly said, "Cuantos necesitas?" "Sólo dos," was Sosa's response. When the MILL official saw Sosa at the game, he raced up to him and asked, "Where did you get your tickets? We could really use more." Sosa replied, "From the Monterrey folks. They have plenty of extra ones." Then Sosa flipped him the bird and walked away.

By two p.m., the start time for the championship game, an estimated 20,000 people, some of whom had arrived as early as 7:30 a.m., packed the stadium and natural amphitheater beyond the outfield fence and bleachers. On the Hill, barely a blade of grass remained uncovered. The throng constituted the largest crowd in Little League World Series history to that point. Dozens also watched out of windows in the hotel on Route 15 that sat atop of the Hill, where many of the MILL parents were staying, including Rogers' parents, James and Letty. All were entertained by the Repasz-Elks Band, a community ensemble founded in 1831 that tooted out the strains of "Take Me Out to the Ball Game" and other patriotic tunes.

The game was broadcast live by Station XET in Monterrey and the Voice of America. It also was videotaped in black-and-white on ABC-TV for *Wide World of Sports.*[60] The TV crew had driven to Williamsport the day before from Atlantic City, the site of the Democratic National Convention, where Lyndon Johnson had been nominated for President. Rogers said of the dozen men setting up cameras around the stadium, "Shortly after we walked onto the field for pre-game drills, they stopped what they were doing to watch us. When we finished, they gave us a standing ovation. It was a thrill that I have reflected on many times."

The ABC-TV play-by-play announcer was Jim McKay, already deep into what would become a renowned career as a broadcaster for a multitude of sports and significant events such as the 1972 Munich Olympics. McKay, who passed away in 2008, is best known for hosting for almost four decades the *Wide World of Sports* series. He gifted us with one of the most memorable sayings in sports history in his introduction of that program, reminding viewers that what lay ahead was "the thrill of victory and the agony of defeat."

The color commentator was Bill Veeck, a fascinating baseball figure who argued there were only two seasons: winter and baseball. In 1947, as owner and team president of the Cleveland Indians, he signed African-American Larry Doby, beginning the integration of the American League. In 1951, Veeck bought a majority interest in the St. Louis Browns. A natural showman, in August of that year he staged the most infamous publicity stunt in baseball history, signing Eddie Gaedel, who stood three feet seven inches tall and weighed sixty-five pounds, to a one-game contract. During a game against the Detroit Tigers, Veeck sent Gaedel to the plate holding a miniature bat to pinch hit in the second game of an August doubleheader with strict instructions not to swing. Wearing elf shoes and "1/8" as his uniform number, and crouching down to present a vertical strike zone estimated at a couple of inches, Gaedel walked on four straight pitches and then was pulled for a pinch runner. It was his only major league at-bat.[61]

The opposing players and coaches trotted onto the field and shook hands before assembling on the foul lines. After Rogers greeted Emilio Roselle Cruz, Monterrey's manager, Sonny Fox, standing at home plate, introduced the starters to the TV audience. He engaged in repartee with some of the kids, asking Johnny Currado why he had the nickname "Mickey Mouse." "Because I'm small and can run fast," Currado retorted. "Well," Fox snapped back, "they'll call you 'Mighty Mouse' if you keep hitting homers." When Greg Klee trotted up, Fox mispronounced his last name as "Clay." Fox then asked, "You made a promise that if your team got to the World Series, you'd what?" Klee shouted, "Win it all!" Fox countered, "We'll see about that."

The national anthem was sung by Eddie Roecker, a local who had been a Broadway star in an earlier era. "Listening to the anthem gave me chills," Donny Quattrochi recalled. "It was like we were at the Olympics with all our family and friends there."

Symbolizing the strong link between the military and Little League, General Albert Wedemeyer threw out the opening pitch. Wedemeyer was a relatively unknown but extremely important World War II Army commander who, as a member of the War Planning Board, had been the main architect of the D-Day invasion. There also was an honorary batter—Harry Humphreys Jr., chairman of U.S. Rubber—who came within an inch from getting beaned by Wedemeyer's wild toss.

In the TV booth, McKay felt compelled to explain to his audience where Staten Island was located. Veeck, smoking beside him, characterized the atmosphere as having "the excitement of a real World Series." He contrasted the styles of the two teams, remarking that Monterrey was a power team that had smashed 27 dingers during tournament play, including seven in a row in one game, while MILL's strengths were pitching and defense. Both McKay and Veeck noted that Monterrey was favored, with McKay stating that, "If Monterrey wins, every factory whistle in the city will blow." After watching the MILL infielders field hard grounders and whip the ball around the bases, Veeck replied, "Don't count Mid-Island out yet. I have a hunch they'll be tough to beat."

As MILL took the field, the umpire barked, "Play ball!" Currado, Ebner, Paul (who turned thirteen that day), Nugent, Yaccarino, and Quattrochi congregated at the mound for the Hail Mary prayer and then ran back to their positions. Game on!

CHAPTER 15
The Best Game There Is

*As I circled the bases, I saw that the infielders looked
defeated, shocked that their star got hit.*

—Danny Yaccarino

GOING INTO THE 1957 Little League World Series,
Monterrey had no reputation to defend and no outside
expectations to satisfy. Their underdog status brought
advantages that were lost on the 1964 squad. Teams that
expect to win tend to focus on maintaining rather than
improving, and can fall into the trap of assuming they do
everything right. A vice that would never be found on a
Rogers-led team.

Yaccarino started strong, fanning Ricardo Moller, the
first Monterrey batter, on a wicked 12-6 curveball that had
him leaning away. "That day," Donny Quattrochi recalled,
"Danny threw his best curveball ever. It looked to the batter
like it was heading toward his head and then would curve
down into my glove. He did that one pitch after another.

Which was good since his fastball wasn't that fast, maybe because it was a really hot day."

After the second batter, Carlos Chavez, flied to Smiechowski in left field, Julian Castillo, also Monterrey's strongest hitter, sauntered to the plate. Castillo was the only returnee from the 1963 Monterrey team that reached Williamsport but lost in the quarterfinals to Duluth, Minnesota.

Every sport has formal rules plus an entire subculture of unwritten ones passed down over the years. In baseball, an attempt by a baserunner on second to observe the signs flashed by the catcher is acceptable, even viewed as customary, on the theory that it's up to the catcher to protect them. Sign stealing via technology is, of course, universally reviled. A notorious example was provided by the 1951 New York Giants. Managed by Leo Durocher, who believed in winning at any cost, the Giants used a telescope, wire, buzzer, and intricate hand signal system to observe and relay the opposing catcher's signs. That assisted Bobby Thompson when he hit his walk-off three-run homer against Ralph Branca to win the decisive contest of a three-game playoff against the Brooklyn Dodgers, in what many regard as the greatest pennant race of all time.[62]

A violation of baseball norms is for a batter to sway his head back as he takes his practice swings and peek in to spot the catcher's signs. Yaccarino's dad Jerry had attended Monterrey's previous two games and told his son that he'd spotted Castillo consistently doing that.

After a foul ball and an inside high curveball for a 1–1 count, Yaccarino requested a timeout and walked off the mound toward home plate. "Danny did that on his own," Rogers emphasized. "He was a tough kid."

Quattrochi stood and stepped toward Yaccarino, assuming he wanted to confer, but Yaccarino marched right past his confused catcher. In the announcer's box, while McKay was puzzled, Veeck guessed the issue. "Castillo," Veeck explained, "is leaning back as he takes his stance in the batter's box, trying to see the catcher's signals." Yaccarino told this to the umpire, who responded, "I noticed that."

The home plate umpire trotted to the Monterrey bench to caution the manager. Veeck observed, "If that happened in the majors, the pitcher wouldn't complain to the umpire. Instead, on the next pitch, the batter would go down fast."

McKay openly wondered how the umpire was able to convey his point to the Monterrey manager and assistant coach, unaware that the Mexican and Japanese teams each had been supplied with an interpreter available in their dugout. "I'm pretty sure," McKay said, "that the umpire doesn't speak Spanish and that the manager and coach don't speak English." Veeck promptly retorted, "Doesn't matter. Umpires are incomprehensible in any language."

As Yaccarino returned to the mound, the Monterrey manager explained to Castillo what the issue was. "That upset him," Yaccarino recalled. "He clearly wasn't accustomed to being challenged about anything he did." Castillo weakly fouled off the next pitch. Then came a 12-6 curveball that froze Castillo before it arched onto the edge of the strike zone. Three up and three down in the top of the first. Greg Klee, with a clear view from center field of Yaccarino's pitching, commented that "Danny was a kind of animal that the Mexicans had never seen. Not just his great curve, but his ability to hit spots. I think they came to Williamsport believing that no one could challenge them. They quickly realized they were in trouble."

Castillo took the mound in the bottom of the first. After Monterrey's quarterfinal contest against Bartlesville, Castillo's hard throwing had landed him in a Williamsport hospital for muscular soreness in his chest and shoulder. "We had heard all week," Klee recollected, "about Castillo. This big kid with a live arm who we had no chance against. Not only was that untrue, but what we came to understand was that he wasn't simply confident—he was arrogant and undisciplined. And that caused him to make mistakes that day that really hurt his team."

As usual, Johnny Currado led off. On a 2–2 count, he lashed a line drive to the right fielder. "That I put so much bat on the ball seemed to shake Castillo up a bit."

Yaccarino stepped to the plate. With the count 2–0, Yaccarino was looking for a fastball and got a high one. "The outfield fence at that time," he explained, "was 200 feet away. I hit the ball 210 feet to right center. It was our team's only homer the entire Series." As Yaccarino rounded the bases, he noticed that Castillo was sobbing on the mound. Reaching home plate, Yaccarino was mobbed by his teammates as if his homer were a walk-off one. "Castillo and the Monterrey team," Yaccarino opined, "weren't the same after that. I kind of felt that the game was over then."

In the top of the second, Yaccarino only gave up a weak grounder to third, striking out the other two batters. Veeck was impressed that Yaccarino would throw his curveball on a full count. "He's a confident kid."

Starting the bottom of the second, Klee beat out a grounder to short. "I never ran so fast. I was so amped up." He took second base on a passed ball. Godnig struck out—he would joke for years about the stigma of striking out on national TV—and Nugent walked. Quattrochi, after failing to bunt successfully, grounded to second. The ball was hit hard enough to turn two, but the shortstop was slow to cover second, and Quattrochi was safe at first.

With a chance to pad the lead, Richie Smiechowski took his turn at bat. On the first pitch, Rogers tested the Monterrey defense by having Quattrochi dash for second on a delayed steal, a tactic he seldom used. In a slick play designed to catch Klee off third base, the catcher threw to Castillo, the pitcher, instead of to second base. Seeing that Klee hadn't strayed far from the base, Castillo turned and tossed to second. His throw, of course, was late, leaving runners at second and third.

With the count 1–1, Smiechowski hit a Baltimore chop that Castillo pounced on. "As soon as Richie hit the ball," Klee admitted, "even though it wasn't a force-play situation, I took off for home plate. There was no doubt in my mind that I could beat Castillo there. But I was wrong." Castillo tagged Klee just before he crossed the plate. The home plate umpire called Klee out and then heard screaming from the MILL bench that Castillo had dropped the ball.

"When I went into my slide," Klee clarified, "he tagged me on my head overly hard, which caused my helmet to spin around and block my vision. Maybe Castillo wanted to punish me for daring to try to score. But that caused him to drop the ball. When I got my bearings, I saw that the umpire reversed his call so I scrambled to touch home plate." A disappointed Castillo kept his composure enough to notice Smiechowski breaking for second and threw him out to end the inning.

To the TV viewer with only one camera angle (behind home plate) and without the benefit of instant replay, and to those in the stands without a side angle, it appeared that Castillo held on to the ball for the requisite amount of time and then perhaps laid it down assuming the inning was over. As the players left the field, Veeck chuckled as he said, "I suppose I should surrender my role as second guesser, but that was a pretty bad call by the umpire." But the umpire's ultimate call was correct. "Thank God for that," Klee reflected, "because I wouldn't have wanted to face Coach Rogers' wrath if I'd been called out."

Three innings in, MILL was ahead 2–0 and Yaccarino had retired all nine batters he faced, with five strikeouts. "It was the Yaccarino show," Smiechowski observed. "He was locked in. We all felt like we were just standing there watching a performance." Veeck remarked that Yaccarino was potential major-league material. "He's got a nice, easy motion and a great curve and live arm with good form and location. There are pro scouts here who will keep his name in the back of their heads until the kid finishes high school." Veeck also was enthralled with the entire MILL squad, opining, "They might be the best ballclub in New York City."

After Yaccarino retired the top of Monterrey's order in the fourth, Sonny Fox corralled Quattrochi for a brief interview as he headed to the dugout. Fox remarked that Yaccarino was sharp and asked Quattrochi if he thought Yaccarino might be getting tired. "No way," Quattrochi responded. When Fox complimented Quattrochi on calling a good game, Quattrochi made clear that "Mr. Rogers gives the signals. I just relay them to Danny." Quattrochi later was teased by his teammates for giving up secrets on national TV.

Starting the bottom of the fourth, Klee slashed the ball into the ground and raced to first fast enough that the third baseman didn't bother with a throw. "Those Baltimore chops," Veeck quipped, "they seem like they're never gonna come down." With Godnig at the plate, Castillo wound up but then stopped and stepped off the rubber. The umpire jumped up and called a balk. As Klee trotted to second base, Castillo flashed a "that-was-not-a-balk" shrug and accompanying grimace that amused McKay and Veeck.

Godnig laid down a soft bunt quickly fielded by Castillo. But the Monterrey player made the mistake of staring Klee back to second for an instant too long and then hastily firing the ball toward the second baseman, covering first. His throw was wild, one of four errors by the Monterrey team. The second baseman, while racing into the runners' lane for the ball, was knocked flat by Godnig, who was furiously trying to beat the throw. As the ball careened off the stands into right field, Klee took third, and Godnig sprinted to second.

Realizing that his star player was off his game, Cruz, the Monterrey manager, switched Castillo to shortstop and sent the shortstop, Roberto Hinojosa, to the pitcher's mound. Veeck joked that Castillo had been "bunted out of the game." Hinojosa, much shorter than Castillo but also hard throwing, gave up a grounder to second by Quattrochi, which allowed Klee to score. The next batter, Nugent, smashed a Hinojosa fastball past the second baseman, plating Godnig with MILL's fourth run.

As the top of the fifth inning began, Yaccarino was six outs from perfection. After the infield throws were completed, Nugent, playing third base, walked the ball to Yaccarino. "You know you've got a perfect game going," Nugent said, violating the sacred baseball tradition that a potential perfect game or no-hitter is not to be spoken about with the pitcher until the game is over. It didn't bother Yaccarino. "I was well aware of the potential to toss a perfect game. And I really wanted it." Rogers sat on the top step of the dugout, pumping his fist and yelling guidance such as "paint the corner," "follow through," and "just miss." As Rogers recalled, "Given the language barrier, I felt I had more freedom to shout out coaching tips." Yaccarino continued his strong pitching, recording his sixth and seventh strikeouts in another 1-2-3 inning.

Between half innings, Yaccarino was interviewed by Sonny Fox. Yaccarino recapped his homer, described how his curveball was working well, and said that Monterrey batters were no longer trying to steal the catcher's signs. As Yaccarino batted to lead off the bottom of the fifth, the camera flashed to his 79-year-old grandma, who had been sick but insisted on attending, sitting pleased in the stands. "Unfortunately, the TV crew messed up," Yaccarino explained. "They actually showed Billy Ebner's grandma."

MILL failed to score in the bottom of the fifth, and Yaccarino's perfect game continued into the top of the sixth inning. The tension in their dugout and among the fans was palpable. Yaccarino had been dominant, allowing only three balls to leave the infield. With the stadium hushed, Yaccarino induced the first batter, Hinojosa, on the first pitch to tap a pop fly to center, easily caught by Klee.

The next batter was a pinch-hitter, Francisco Moreno, Monterrey's smallest player. As Moreno approached the plate, Rogers leaned out of the dugout toward Mike Sosa, sitting nearby. "Mike," Rogers barked, "what do you got on this kid?" To Rogers' annoyance, Sosa just shrugged. "Moreno," Eddie Sosa explained, "hadn't played in the previous two games, so my dad didn't know anything about him."

Moreno worked the count to 3–2. Rogers relayed to Quattrochi that he wanted Yaccarino to use his 12-6 curveball. Rogers nervously yelled out, "Hang in there, Danny!" Yaccarino wound up and threw, but his release point was too high and the ball came in at eye level. Moreno let it go for ball four. Yaccarino kicked the mound dirt in frustration, and the crowd groaned as Morena trotted to first. "I was trying too much," Yaccarino later reflected. "For the first time that game, I got anxious and hung the curve." Over a half century later, Rogers shook his head at the mention of that pitch. "I blame myself. I should have called for a fastball."

In the announcer's booth, McKay turned to Veeck and asked, "Think that will mess up Yaccarino psychologically?" "I don't think in the least," Veeck replied. Veeck was correct, as Yaccarino fanned the next batter, Juan Garza, his eighth punchout, on a trademark curveball.

On the first pitch to Roberto Muller, the leadoff batter, the game ended with a weak comebacker to the mound. Yaccarino's no-hitter was the third one by a winning U.S. pitcher in the World Series championship game over a five-year-period.[63]

Milliseconds after closing his glove on the final out, Ebner leaped in the air as Rogers dashed out of the dugout with fist raised. Yaccarino, his hat flying, ran into Rogers' arms and then was swarmed by his teammates. The players' fathers rushed onto the field, two holding a banner proclaiming MILL as world champions. McKay characterized Yaccarino as "just about the happiest boy in America," and commented, "Looking at this scene, all I can think of is when Bobby Thompson hit his home run in 1951." Veeck, with deep emotion in his voice, mused that "this excitement and enthusiasm shows why baseball is the best game there is."

Amid the pandemonium, Sonny Fox again interviewed Yaccarino, who explained how he'd hung the curveball to Moreno that was ball four. Prompted by Fox, Yaccarino announced he wanted to become a pro ballplayer when he grew up. Fox summoned over Yaccarino's father, who spoke of how proud he was. "That Sonny asked my dad to join me for an interview on national TV," Yaccarino reminisced, "was a wonderful touch that I appreciated more as I got older." Yaccarino would be deluged with autograph seekers, photographers, newspaper reporters, and well-wishers, and interviewed by several radio stations, including one from Mexico.

The new world champions had outscored their rivals 78–9 in a dominant thirteen-game tournament stretch. In Williamsport, their opposition crossed the plate only twice in three games.

Since 1964, seven other teams from the five boroughs have reached Williamsport, with Mid-Island achieving that challenging goal in 2006 and 2018.[64] But none have advanced to the championship game, let alone won it all.[65] The 1964 MILL team had become and would remain legend, and the accolades quickly began to flow.

Team members holding trophies in Williamsport

"MID-ISLAND'S OWN"
1964 Little League World Champions
Back Row (left to right) - Bill Rogers, Bob Nagent,
Greg Klee, Don Yaccarino, Frank Higgins, Billy Hig-
gins, Gary Kresge, Coach - Bob Klee, John Porcell.
Bottom (left to right) - John Currado, Rich
Smiechowski, Mickie Wicinski, Michael Triano, Dom
Quattrochi, Jeff Paul, Ed Godnig.

Team photo in Williamsport–"Billy Higgins" should read "Billy Ebner" and "Don Yaccarino" should read "Dan Yaccarino"

CHAPTER 16
Lucy and Casey

I felt like a soldier coming home from war to a hero's welcome.

—Jeff Paul

THE RAUCOUS CELEBRATION and assorted interviews now over, every kid knew what must follow. They hustled back to their cabin, donned swim trunks, and made a bee line to the pool. For the first time all summer, the boys swam. When Rogers arrived, they pushed him, fully clothed, into the pool. Later, they re-lived the game as they watched ABC's broadcast on tape delay, making fun of each other as they sat around the TV.

The next morning, Sunday, August 30, each player received a custom-made Louisville Slugger bat, a Little League World Series logo jacket, and a trophy. Then the team boarded a bus for their return home. "The streets in our neighborhood were lined with people cheering and waving to us and holding signs," Jeff Paul recalled. Signs hung on trees and poles in their neighborhoods hailed their world championship. One, on Perry Avenue, read, "Our hero, Jeff Paul."

That night, the MILL players joined the other seven World Series teams, a total of 112 boys, for a three-night stay at C.W. Post college in Brooksville, Long Island, as guests of the *Daily News.* On Monday, they all were treated to a VIP (no waiting in lines) whirlwind tour of World's Fair pavilions and rides. "It was nice getting to go to the Fair," Greg Klee observed, "but that was in our backyard. We were disappointed because it was traditional for the championship team to travel to Washington and visit with the President. Guess they thought, wrongly, that going to the World's Fair was better."

*Members of several 1964 Little League World Series
teams in front of the New York State pavilion*

Little Leaguers meet Lucille Ball

The next day, the players returned to the Fair and toured a flurry of other pavilions. The Fair, a magical wonderland in a time before Disney World, attracted global celebrities. Tuesday, September 1, happened to be "Lucy Day." Hordes of screaming camera-clicking fairgoers waited at each of the stops made by Lucille Ball, then one of the most popular and well-known persons in the world, who arrived along with her Borscht Belt comedian husband, Gary Morton. They were joined by Hedda Hopper, the notorious Hollywood gossip columnist, wearing one of her trademark ostentatious hats—this one white, wide-brimmed, and fluffy.[66]

"The highlight of that day for me," Richie Smiechowski recounted, "was our private session with Lucy and having our picture taken with her.[67] Many decades later, I really impressed my daughter by showing her that photo."

In the late afternoon, the boys walked over to Shea Stadium, adjoining the Fair site, where the Mets would face the San Francisco Giants that night. The MILL team was invited to eat dinner in the Diamond Club, one of the stadium's two restaurants. "It was so cool," Klee said, "being in this fancy restaurant with a great view of the field. We were sitting there for a while, and then waiters paraded in with plates of lobster tails. Us kids are looking at each other thinking, 'What the hell are they?' We asked for grill cheese sandwiches."

Before the game, the boys were allowed to wander the field and dugouts. Billy Ebner meandered over to the batting cage, where the Giants were taking batting practice. Standing there was Willie McCovey, a fearsome power hitter who, when he retired in 1980, ranked second only to Babe Ruth in career home runs among left-handed batters. "I did a double take. I'd never seen a person of that size in my life."

Casey Stengel, the Mets manager and one of the most beloved, well-known figures in baseball history, chatted up the boys in the dugout.[68] "Seeing Casey up close," Bobby Nugent explained, "was more awe inspiring than meeting Lucy. She never hit a home run or struck out a batter."

Stengel was famous for his implausible double-talk, dubbed "Stengelese," such as "there comes a time in every man's life, and I've had plenty of them," which the sportswriter Red Smith once likened listening to as trying to "pick up quicksilver with boxing gloves." At one point, Stengel and Yaccarino sat next to each other. "He talked to me for a while," Yaccarino recalled, "but I had no idea what he was saying."

Yaccarino and Donny Quattrochi were summoned to the broadcast booth to be interviewed by Mets announcer Ralph Kiner, a Hall of Fame outfielder who would go on to have a remarkable 53-season broadcasting career. Joining them was Bill Shea, a prominent lawyer instrumental in bringing National League baseball back to the City with the New York Mets, which led to his being the stadium's namesake. Regarding Quattrochi, Shea said to Kiner, "If Cannizzaro [the Mets starting catcher] wasn't going so good right now, I'd suggest to Casey that he sign Donny."

Before game time, the MILL players were introduced individually, and then each trotted to the pitcher's mound to fierce applause from the crowd of 45,000. Yaccarino, who had been given the opportunity to meet with Willie Mays and Alvin Dark, the Giants skipper, was announced last. "To this day," he reminisced, "I get chills thinking about the deafening blare of that standing ovation and all the airhorns that went off as I ran onto the field."

The game, won by the Mets 4–1, was made memorable in major league history with the debut of Masanori Murakami, a side-armed reliever who, as a teenager, had reverted to his natural left-handed inclination. That night, Murakami became the first Japanese-born man to play in the Major Leagues.[69]

MILL players at Shea Stadium

On Wednesday, September 2, the boys were honored at Staten Island Borough Hall at St. George. Borough President Albert Maniscalco, a decades-long force in Staten Island's political and civic life, welcomed them with a speech in which he declared, "The Verrazzano-Narrows Bridge will put us on the map. But these kids have done it already!"

The boys then were whisked away in a motorcade of convertibles on a winding path through the East Shore, Great Kills, North Shore, South Shore, and West Shore Little League neighborhoods. Along the way, well-wishers raced out into the street to shake their hands and ask for autographs.

The procession ended at Cascio Field, where the crowd in the stands overflowed onto the infield. The players marched in as conquering heroes, accompanied by officials from the American Legion and Veterans of Foreign Wars and the Thunderbird Drum and Bugle Corps. "We were celebrities," Yaccarino recalled. "Particularly me. One man gave me a $20 bill to sign. I was feeling bad that I got so much of the attention." After William Cascio, a builder on whose property the field was located, was introduced, officials from the Staten Island Rod and Gun Club awarded Rogers and team a five-foot trophy and MILL officials presented the players with an oversized cake in the shape of a baseball diamond. Two dads, Phil Ebner and Bob Higgins, unfurled the "Little League 1964 Champions" banner that had been presented to the team in Williamsport.

As the fans screamed, the team was ushered to a podium on the field. Maniscalco read a proclamation honoring them. Bobby Nugent then handed him a baseball signed by all players. "I was nervous," Nugent admitted, "and I said to him 'I'd like to present to you a signed, autographed baseball from the team.' I realized right away that 'signed' and 'autographed' were redundant. But, of course, no one cared except me."

The day-long celebration had been one the likes of which the MILL boys, and few others, had ever experienced. Until the following day.

CHAPTER 17
Canyon of Heroes

My mom was in seventh heaven. She got all dressed up, and received a bouquet along with the other moms. Till her final days, she thought of that time with great affection.

—Richie Smiechowski

THE IDEA FOR A ticker-tape parade was inspired by the stock ticker, a machine invented in the late 19th century that tracked and then conveyed over telegraph lines the value of stocks being traded, stamping prices on one-inch-wide paper strips that flowed continuously. The tape that spit out of the machines would gather in piles on the floor.

The first ticker-tape parade through Manhattan's "Canyon of Heroes," in the Financial District, occurred spontaneously in October 1886 after the dedication of the Statue of Liberty by President Grover Cleveland. As the commemorative parade wound its way up Broadway, observers from offices above showered down ticker-tape from their windows.

Soon after that, in recognition of that event's popularity, city officials institutionalized the practice for triumphant commemorations in honor of kings, queens, popes, presidents, foreign dignitaries, military leaders, astronauts, adventurers, Olympians, and other notables as well as for championships by a New York City sports team.[70]

A parade for the MILL team was suggested by Bill Shea, Chairman of the Mayor's Baseball Committee and Albert Maniscalco, and approved by Robert Wagner Jr., who was nearing the end of his third and final term as mayor. Wagner had been in his first term in October 1957 when the Brooklyn Dodgers and New York Giants each announced it was moving out of the city, starting the following season, to the promised land of California. Wagner was widely blamed for the two crushing losses, along with Robert Moses, by then New York City Parks Commissioner, and the two team owners, Walter O'Malley of the Dodgers and Horace Stoneham of the Giants.

In the case of the Giants, New York's oldest baseball team, their home field was the fourth incarnation of the original Polo Grounds, opened in 1876, which had been built for the sport of polo. The Polo Grounds possessed a storied baseball history, including being the field where Babe Ruth first wore his Yankee uniform in 1920 and where Bobby Thompson's "Shot Heard 'Round the World" occurred in 1951.

The stadium, located in Coogan's Bluff, a promontory near the western shore of the Harlem River in the Washington Heights neighborhood of upper Manhattan, across from Yankee Stadium, was by 1957 an aging ballpark. Stoneham was concerned about the plummet in attendance, caused in part because the vicinity had become crime ridden. He complained to Wagner, telling him that the Giants couldn't guarantee their box-seat customers safety from armed robberies during night games. Stoneham asked the city for a new municipal stadium, but Wagner, like Moses a non-sports fan at heart, took little action. Then Moses announced that he wanted to build public housing on the Polo Grounds site and cavalierly suggested to Stoneham that the Giants move into Yankee Stadium. An irate Stoneham retorted that such doubling-up was not the custom in baseball. Believing that the City intended to seize the Polo Grounds, Stoneham began looking outside New York for a place to call home.

As for the Dodgers, O'Malley insisted that Ebbets Field, also situated in an increasingly unsafe neighborhood and without parking facilities, was obsolete. O'Malley wanted to stay in Brooklyn, hoping to build a stadium at the Atlantic Avenue terminal at the junction of Flatbush and Atlantic Avenues (where the Barclays Center now stands), an ideal location as numerous subway lines and the Long Island Railroad converge there. O'Malley asked Wagner to have the city condemn and buy the parcel of "slum land" for the purpose of selling or leasing it to him. Wagner remained apathetic, and Moses refused to use taxpayers' money to underwrite a new facility. Moses, who hated public transportation, preferring the automobile, was determined to shift the Dodgers out of urban Brooklyn and into what was then semi-suburban Queens. He tried to sell O'Malley on the notion of building a stadium in Flushing Meadows, Queens, located right off major highways and served by an elevated subway line. The Dodgers owner rejected this, insisting that if his team stayed in the City, it would be in Brooklyn.

Wagner, stung by harsh criticism in 1957 from millions of local baseball fans, vowed to lure another team to New York. After five years, and with the help of Shea, whose ties to the circles of power in New York politics and professional sports ran deep, Wagner convinced the National League to form the Mets as a New York team. Wagner continued to seek opportunities to display his support of the national pastime. The MILL championship handed him a golden one.

On Thursday, September 3, the MILL team members, wearing their uniforms, rode the Staten Island Ferry to lower Manhattan. Awaiting them were open white Cadillac convertible limos with bright red interiors for a journey in style from South Ferry to City Hall. Two 50-piece bands, dozens of mounted policemen, the Fire Department's color guard, and a bevy of dignitaries joined a crowd estimated at 25,000 for the celebration.

Leading the procession were Yaccarino, Ebner, and Greg Klee, perched high in the back of their limo—a magical moment for even the loftiest of souls. Sitting in front of them were Shea and Maniscalco, with famed WNBC-TV reporter Gabe Pressmen, microphone in hand, trotting alongside. "I'd never been in a luxurious vehicle like that," Klee reminisced. "I'd also never been on Broadway, and there I was, at the head of the parade with a clear shot of the incredible crowds going nuts over us. Made me feel like we were the Yankees." Yaccarino admitted, "As a twelve-year-old, I didn't understand the magnitude of it all. It was just another event. But a pretty damn big one."

Rogers, Bob Klee, and the other players followed. "My dad," Klee explained, "beamed with pride for me and all the other kids, who he considered his extended sons. The fact that he was a Transit Authority employee made it even more special for him. The very city that he worked for was now honoring him and all of us."

The last limos in the convoy housed the players' mothers. "It was a wonderful touch to invite our moms," Jeff Paul observed. "Our dads had been most involved during the season with the moms in the background. Now they had the spotlight."

As the limos crawled up Broadway, the sidewalks were jammed from barrier to building. Steamers, confetti, and all sorts of paper rained down from open windows. Construction workers perched on overhead ledges cheered and applauded. Skywriters zoomed overhead, although their messages were blocked by the buildings. Joe Nugent was among the spectators. "I was jealous," he admitted. "My little brother is having teenage girls screaming at him and begging for an autograph, and I can't even get a date."

Upon arriving at City Hall, the team members each were handed an official "City Key" tie clip by Mayor Wagner. With the Yankees locked in a tight pennant race and the Mets hapless, Wagner presciently announced, "I'm afraid

Danny handing Mayor Wagner an autographed ball

you may be the only world championship baseball team we have this year."

*

The following weeks would be a whirlwind, including a helicopter ride, during which the pilot asked Yaccarino for his autograph, and a three-hour Circle Line cruise around Manhattan. The team was invited for a guest weekend at the now-defunct Grossinger's (the Catskills resort that inspired "Kellerman's Mountain Resort" in the 1987 film *Dirty Dancing*), where Yaccarino wound up gliding across the dance floor with Hollywood star Kim Novak. Smiechowski characterized that September as "wine and dine" month. "One day, we went to a synagogue in Elizabeth, New Jersey, for bagels and coffee. Another day, we went to a youth club in Brooklyn for pizza and soda. And it seemed like once a week we saw Maniscalco. After a while, it got to be too much."

Maniscalco wasn't the only politician seeking to associate himself with New York's newest favorites. New York Governor Nelson Rockefeller, who earlier that year had unsuccessfully sought the Republican Party nomination for president (and who would, a decade later, be appointed U.S. vice president under Gerald Ford), invited the team to visit him in Albany. "He was quite jovial," Ebner recalled. "We were running around his desk and office and all he kept saying, while looking at a TV camera, was, 'How wonderful is this!' A true old school politician."

One night, the team feasted at Staten Island's historic Tavern on the Green, on Hylan Boulevard in New Dorp, then in its heyday.[71] The restaurant was Staten Island's best-known site for political dinners and lunches, affairs for community and charitable organizations, and countless family and other social events. Celebrities would routinely drop in. Tavern on the Green was where Bobby Thompson, the "Staten Island Scot" who was born in Glasgow, chose to have dinner on October 3, 1951 after having hit his historic homer hours before. "We were blown away by the elegance of the place," Jeff Paul recollected. "None of us were used to fancy anything."

On Friday, September 11, the MILL team was transported to Yankee Stadium, where they dined in the club restaurant. Before the game between the Yankees and Minnesota Twins, Yaccarino was interviewed by Red Barber, the colorful Mississippi-born announcer known for his many catchphrases such as "back, back, back" to describe a long fly ball with home-run potential. Then the boys were escorted to the Yankee dugout. "We got to hang out there for fifteen minutes," Eddie Godnig recalled. "I was one of the first guys in, and I quickly grabbed Mantle's helmet, with the number "7" painted on the dark blue, and plopped it on. Of course, it was far too big for me. Then I snatched his bat, walked in front of the dugout, and swung it repeatedly. The fans were yelling at me, 'What the hell are you doing?' But I didn't care."

Greg Klee was a huge fan of The Mick as well. "When our time came to leave, they took us through the dugout and down the runway. As I took a step down in the dugout, Mantle walked past. My eyes blew up like balloons. I was so mesmerized that I accidentally stepped on his foot. He just laughed and kept going."

As at Shea Stadium, the boys were walked to the pitcher's mound and introduced to the throng. "I looked up as the place went wild," Rogers recalled. "You couldn't see the folks in the upper levels because of the bright lights. The best part was that the kids were beside themselves."

For Paul, the month's highlight came on September 30, when he and his parents were guests of the AFL-CIO's International Association of Bridge, Structural, and Ornamental Iron Workers Local 40 (known as the "Mohawk Ironworkers") at the night half of a doubleheader in the Bronx between the Yankees and Detroit Tigers. "The stadium was packed. Before the game, my parents and I were ushered into the Yankee dugout. Once again, I felt as if I were in heaven, getting to roam around before the players arrived. At one point, right in front of me was Mantle's helmet. It was like seeing the True Cross."

In 1964, talk of the World Series, still the country's premier sporting event, dominated conversations in millions of households. Reporting on the games became front-page news. During weekday afternoon games, school truancy skyrocketed. Office workers would take frequent breaks to gather in small knots around transistor radios or TVs. On Wall Street, stock and bond trading slowed.

Johnny Currado returned with his father to Yankee Stadium in the afternoon of Saturday, October 10, to attend game three of the 1964 Yankee-Cardinal World Series, which was tied one game apiece. "The Yankees invited one member of our team to attend and throw out the first ball." Currado explained. "We all picked names out of a hat, and I won. It's the only thing of value I've ever won by sheer luck in my life. I got a standing ovation when I was introduced. I didn't throw the first pitch from the mound, however. Instead, I stood behind home plate and threw to

Elston Howard, the Yankee catcher. He and Jim Bouton, the Yankee starter who played Little League baseball himself, signed the ball."

Johnny and his father, along with 67,000 other fans, watched drama unfold. In the bottom of the ninth, with the scored tied 1–1, 38-year-old knuckleballer Barney Schultz was called on to relieve Cardinal hurler Curt Simmons, who had been pulled for a pinch hitter after pitching masterfully and driving in the Cards only run. Mantle, batting first in the inning, had produced another stellar season in 1964 with 35 home runs and 111 RBIs while leading the American League in on-base percentage. But he suffered from serious knee and shoulder problems and couldn't throw or run well anymore. The breakdown of Mantle's body reflected, in a sense, the collapse of a remarkable Yankee dynasty that had seen it participate in fifteen World Series since 1947, winning ten of them.

In a time before the designated-hitter option, Mantle played right field. It was his error in the fifth inning, allowing a ball to run through his legs, that led to the Cardinals tying the game. Now he sought redemption. Standing in the dugout, Mantle watched intensely as Schultz threw his warmup knuckleballs. Walking over to Bouton at the water cooler, he announced, "I'm gonna hit one outta here." As Mantle strode to the batter's box, he passed Elston Howard, crouching in the on-deck circle. "Ellie," Mantle insisted, "you might as well go back to the dugout because this game is over."

The first pitch to Mantle, a knuckler that didn't dance or flutter, came in knee-high down the middle. Mantle, a lethal low-ball hitter batting left-handed, turned and crushed it. Schultz took one quick look over his shoulder and walked off the mound as the ball sailed into the third deck in right field and the stadium erupted. The Yankees went up 2–1 in the Series, with Mantle breaking Babe Ruth's record by hitting his sixteenth homer in World Series play.

"My dad and I were sitting in the reporters' box," Currado recalled. "We'd been invited to the Yankee locker room after the game. Once Mantle homered, we started walking down. But then someone came and told us that it was just too crazy a celebration going on to allow us in. I can only imagine."

The tributes and festivities gradually faded away. But the fairytale account of the 1964 MILL team endures. "On Staten Island, they're like the 'Hoosiers,'" Jay Price quipped. "The story never gets old."

CHAPTER 18
Aftermath

*Someone told me, 'I don't care how long you live on Staten
Island. In your obituary, it'll say you were from Brooklyn.'*
                                                    —Pat Salmon

THE MILL LITTLE League World Series victory was an
unabashed positive for Staten Island. That, however, was
not the universal view regarding the Verrazzano-Narrows
Bridge. One homeowner, Richard Neville of Mariners
Harbor, described it as "a two-faced woman. At a distance,
she's beautiful, but, up close, she's ugly. The bridge has
not meant progress, only change, and I mean change for
the worse."

The bridge, the last great public-works project overseen
by Robert Moses, opened on Saturday, November 21, 1964
at 11 a.m. on an exquisite, cloudless day. With Moses presid-
ing over the ceremonies, 1,500 invited guests gathered to
witness a ribbon cutting at the 92nd St. Brooklyn entrance
to the bridge. They then traveled in a limousine motorcade

over the bridge as fireboats chugged through the Narrows spraying high plumes of water in salute. Cannons were fired from the U.S. Army forts on either side.

Later, a flag was raised at the Staten Island plaza, and Jeanette Scovetti of the Metropolitan Opera sang the National Anthem. Rockefeller, Wagner, and Maniscalco all spoke. At three p.m. the Verrazzano-Narrows Bridge was officially opened to traffic. In the first hour, an estimated 5,000 cars crossed its span, each paying a toll of fifty cents. In the bridge's first full year of operation, the volume of seventeen million vehicles well overshot estimates. The Verrazzano's popularity prompted the Triborough Bridge and Tunnel Authority to increase capacity with the addition in 1967 of a six-lane lower level.

Much of the Island was bulldozed by land developers and littered with housing complexes. Pat Salmon remembers the farms in and around Bulls Head with great fondness. "They quickly disappeared. Farmers couldn't resist the prices and, in many cases, their children didn't want to continue the business. On a single farm, dozens if not hundreds of mother-daughter houses could be built."

The bridge triggered a mass migration to Staten Island that quickly doubled its population, with the majority arriving from Brooklyn. As described by Thomas Matteo, Staten Island historian, "Brooklyn was like a bottle that was bulging at the seams. That cork popped, and we had a flood on Staten Island." But the dream of many newcomers of enjoying an idyllic suburban lifestyle was washed away by their own onslaught. Jay Price's summary was that Staten

Island "expanded too intensely, too quickly, and with too little civic planning, becoming Brooklyn but without the charm."

There was an element of white flight involved. As Salmon explained, "Realtors in Brooklyn scared residents about incoming minorities so they could buy up properties cheaply." Salmon's own family moved to Staten Island when she was four. "Even though I essentially grew up on the Island, I was thought of as a Brooklynite, who many native Staten Islanders instinctively disliked."

Legal trouble for Staten Island brewed. Since 1898, each of the five borough presidents held an equal number of votes, regardless of population, on the Board of Estimate, the city's governmental body. In March 1989, the U.S. Supreme Court unanimously ruled that the Board of Estimate was unconstitutional on the grounds that Brooklyn, the city's most populous borough, enjoyed no more representation than Staten Island, the city's least populous borough, an arrangement that violated the Fourteenth Amendment's Equal Protection Clause and the "one man, one vote" principle.

In response, the Board of Estimate was abolished, leaving Staten Island entitled to only three members of a new 51-member City Council. This loss in representation prompted Staten Island politicians to push for a measure, ultimately passed by the New York State Legislature and signed by Governor Mario Cuomo, authorizing a study of secession from New York City. In November 1993, a non-binding referendum to secede was approved by Staten Island voters by a 2–1 margin. But the move was blocked by New York's State Assembly, which determined that the necessary approval needed to come from the city's government.

Dubbed "Stexit" after Britain's decision to quit the European Union, the effort remains alive to this day. If approved, Staten Island's succession would be the largest municipal separation in the United States since the Civil War.

CHAPTER 19
Reflections

*Memory is a time machine. I am forever in the summer of
1964.*

—Eddie Godnig

WHAT IS THE IMPACT ON a person when his "fifteen
minutes of fame" occurs at age twelve or younger, when
mature, fulsome perspective is impossible? How did the team
members fare in adulthood, and what was the impact of the
Little League World Series championship on their lives?

These days, the MILL players are spread out across the
country—from Florida to Alaska. Few still live in Staten
Island. But, every August, their minds drift back to 1964.

As with most of them, for Johnny Currado, baseball
remained in his blood, with Little League acting as a step-
ping stone to the Babe Ruth league, high school varsity,
American Legion ball, and beyond. At Port Richmond High
School, he starred at second base, playing along with Klee,
Paul, Quattrochi, Smiechowski, and Yaccarino. The MILL

crew formed the core of the Port Richmond team that captured the Staten Island High School baseball championship in 1969, their senior year, in a playoff against Monsignor Farrell High School (with Yaccarino and Nugent facing off against each other for the only time in their lives).

Currado received a full scholarship offer from New York University. "I wanted to join a big-name baseball program like Arizona State. But the year I graduated, NYU's team qualified for the College World Series. That and the full tuition ride sold me on them."

Currado played second base on the NYU varsity team for four years. In 1971, as a sophomore, he was named the most valuable player in the Atlantic Coast Baseball League. He was selected as a member of the U.S. National baseball team that traveled to Italy to compete in the Intercontinental Cup Tournament, finishing third behind Japan and Puerto Rico. "There were some top-notch players on that team," he recalled, "including Bill Almon and Rick Cerrone, who both made it to the majors." Currado roomed with Ed Ford, the son of legendary Yankee pitcher Whitey Ford. "It was a fun-loving group. At one point, there was an outbreak of cholera so we brushed our teeth with wine."

Currado held hopes of being drafted by a major league team after graduating. "The problem was my height. I was only five feet, six inches, and that put off teams. It really hurt when I wasn't drafted at all." The majors' oversight of Currado bothered his teammates as well. "At every level he competed," Greg Klee pointed out, "Johnny was a winner. How could it be that no one was willing to take a chance on him?" Joe Nugent remarked, "Johnny, in my view, had big-league talent and could have been, and should have been, another Freddie Patek. But he never got the opportunity." Currado enjoys the distinction of competing on both national championship baseball and softball teams. In 1975, he played shortstop for Silvestri's Service Station, a Staten Island team that earned the first official American Softball Association national championship. "Staten Island was a hotbed of softball then, with a lot of good teams. I became hooked on the sport and played for many more years. Our team won the national championship again in 1983 and 1984. In 1984, I was named the MVP of the tournament."[72]

After spending most of his business career at Allstate Insurance, coincidentally a sponsor of Little League base-ball, Currado retired as a senior sales manager in the executive staff. He and his second wife Barbara now live in St. Petersburg, Florida. Between them, they have four children and four grandchildren.

Looking back on the championship summer, Currado shared, "With the benefit of hindsight, the best aspect of it was the life lessons I learned, like working hard, commit-ting to something, having a passion, that body language is important, and that practice and preparation are criti-cal. Which is why the MILL experience has helped me my whole life."

Human nature being what it is, Danny Yaccarino couldn't let go. "I was one pitch away from perfection. It shouldn't have bothered me, but it did. And, in high school, the guys rode me about it."

Yaccarino revealed, "After we came home from Williamsport, I received dozens of letters from girls around the country. Things like 'You're so cute,' and 'I'd love to meet you.' My dad answered every letter on his typewriter. Years later, when I was really into girls, I wished for letters like that."

Jim Bouton once commented, "A ballplayer spends a good piece of his life gripping a baseball, and in the end it turns out that it was the other way around all the time." Yaccarino aggressively pursued his vision of becoming a major leaguer and came closest of all the team members to achieving it. Signed in 1969 out of Port Richmond High School by Baltimore Orioles' scout Joe Torre, Senior (the father of major leaguers Joe and Frank Torre and a former New York City detective), he was sent to Aberdeen, South Dakota, to play on the Orioles' Single A affiliate. "It was culture shock for me, going from Staten Island to South Dakota at age eighteen. But in a good, learning way."

Yaccarino would reach the Double-A level and play with future major leaguers Enos Cabell, Wayne Garland, and Larry Milbourne. "One game, the opposing pitcher was Don Gullett, who was with the Sioux Falls Packers [and who would go on to become a star for the Cincinnati Reds and New York Yankees and appear in six World Series]. Even though we had a good hitting team, he punched out 19 of 21 batters he faced. I got up against him but had no chance. He threw a 95 miles per hour fastball and a wicked bender. Now that was real talent."

Yaccarino lasted just two seasons in pro ball, tabbed "the Little League guy" wherever he pitched and ridden by bench jockeys. "People anticipated perfection from me, and I demanded it from myself. An absurd expectation, of course. Because I wasn't content to be who I was, I had no place to go but down."

One day, Joe Torre invited Yaccarino to observe pregame drills on the Shea Stadium field. "After watching Tom Seaver and Nolan Ryan warm up, I decided right there that if that's what big-league pitchers look like, I didn't have much of a chance. If I knew then that they were both going to the Hall of Fame, maybe I wouldn't have felt so over-matched."

After baseball, Yaccarino embarked on a number of careers, including scouting for the Orioles, owning and running race horses, working as a salesman for Frank Torre's sporting goods store, acting as a union representative in the school bus industry, and teaching golf. Divorced and with two sons and three grandkids, Yaccarino now lives in West Palm Beach. "Golf is great, but baseball is magical to me. Always will be."

Yaccarino credits the confident attitude instilled in him and his teammates—the conviction, if not the certainty, that one can achieve any goal with focus and determination—with helping him in his decade-plus long battle with cancer. "The mind is a powerful thing. I learned that when I was a kid and have always benefitted from it."

When asked about the summer of '64, Yaccarino admits to still being uncomfortable about receiving so much of the limelight. "The championship truly was a team effort, as all baseball championships must be." Yaccarino added, "In any event, my fondest memories aren't about winning at Williamsport or the ticker-tape parade or my no-hitter or meeting all the celebrities, as great as all that was. The recollections that warm my heart are about the practices, the games themselves, and the closeness of the team as we competed together. Those were the most joyful parts of the entire experience."

Bobby Nugent played baseball for many more years, although he also indulged in another passion, basketball, and excelled at that. In middle school, Nugent was named the best eighth-grade basketball player on Staten Island. As a freshman at Monsignor Farrell, he averaged 25 points per game and was named to the all-New York City high school freshman team. "That was a huge deal," his brother Joe explained, "because the other four starters were from big-name high schools in the other boroughs."

Monsignor Farrell was an all-boys high school. "I received a partial baseball scholarship offer from St. Michael's College in Vermont. When I looked at their brochure, I saw women in it, so I was happy. Then I get there and find out there were 1,300 men and 23 women. It was the first year the school went coed. But it got better after that."

Nugent would pitch for four years at St. Michael's and toss the only perfect game in school history. He was scouted in college by Bill Monbouquette, who had been a right-handed pitcher for several major league teams in the 1950s and '60s, noted for pitching a no-hitter in 1962 as a member of the Boston Red Sox. "Monbouquette told me," Nugent recalled, "that every game he watched me pitch, he was impressed that I threw the ball exactly where it should be thrown. Unfortunately, he was looking for someone big who could throw 95 plus. That wasn't me."

After college, Nugent worked for Coca-Cola USA as an account executive, moving around the country as he advanced up the corporate chain.[73] Nugent and his wife Kathleen, who he met at St. Michael's on the day he threw his perfect game, have three daughters and three grandkids and now live in Venice, Florida.

Speaking about the MILL team comes second nature to Nugent. "Throughout my entire thirty-plus-year career, people I interacted with at conventions, golf outings, and meetings were impressed by my being on a world-championship team. Even women, because so many had brothers or other family members who played Little League. It was a hell of an icebreaker that helped facilitate conversations and a lot of business."

For Donny Quattrochi, high school marked the end of his baseball career. Having pulled a low number in the lottery for the Vietnam War, and given his patriotism, he opted to join the Armed Forces. "My dad had served as a shipman in the Navy during World War II. He said to me, 'Do you want to sleep in a tent in the jungle or in a rack on a ship?' So, I joined the Navy." Quattrochi served for two years in active duty and six years in reserve. "I lucked out, not having been sent to Vietnam. Then I lucked out again, meeting my wife Maria while on a submarine tender docked in Rota, Spain. We got married in Madrid when I was twenty-one and she was only eighteen. She spoke little English at the time and I spoke almost no Spanish. When I asked her father for permission to marry his daughter, I had to have a friend write a letter in Spanish for me."

After his Navy service, Quattrochi returned to Staten Island and joined the U.S. Postal Service, where he worked for four decades. He and his wife raised a son and daughter. A heavy smoker, Maria died at age 49 from lung cancer. Quattrochi, who has two granddaughters, never remarried and remained living on Staten Island.

He often reflects back on the summer of '64. "We weren't worldly and didn't understand how amazing it was. We're still the only kids to ever get a ticker-tape parade down Broadway. It meant more to me later on. At the time, it was more of a thrill for our parents. What I'm most glad for is the bond among us that has lasted through the decades."

Jeff Paul received a full athletic scholarship to Long Island University, where he played baseball for four years. Afterward, Paul took on several teaching jobs while obtaining a master's degree, before enlisting in the New York Fire Department. Paul now lives in Staten Island with his second wife, Betty. The Pauls spend much of their time with their twelve combined grandchildren, one of whom, Sienna, they share with the author and his wife.

Paul often quips that he becomes famous every August. Thinking back on August 1964, he admitted, "It was overwhelming. I've always said, I wish it had happened when

I was sixteen or older. I would've enjoyed it more. My dad often would mention it to others with pride, which I enjoyed hearing. Now, when I talk about it, Betty tells me I've turned my fifteen minutes of fame into fifteen hours."

As did millions of boys, Greg Klee dreamed of replacing Mantle as the Yankee's center fielder. But after playing high school baseball, he went on to other pursuits, including decades as a corrections officer. Following his retirement, Klee and his wife Samantha moved to Maryville, Tennessee. "I couldn't take the congestion anymore."

Klee has spoken little over the years about his participation on a world-championship team. But he ponders it a great deal. "I often wonder, why me? Most people don't have that moment at any age. Plus, I got to enjoy it with family and friends. I particularly feel blessed to have spent those weeks so close to my dad."

Richie Smiechowski also played on the 1965 MILL All-Star team (not coached by Bill Rogers), which lost in extra innings to West Shore in the Staten Island championship game. Smiechowski went on to play college baseball and basketball at Wagner College, graduating with a B.S. in chemistry. He then focused on his career and family, raising three kids with his wife Candice. They live in Reston, Virginia, where Smiechowski runs a technology sales and business development company. "I get a kick out of showing the DVD of the championship game to my three grandkids. It's something that really impresses them. I've always been able to put that moment into perspective. It was just one of many things I'm proud of, like raising a family and starting a business. And those achievements have a lot more breadth."

Billy Ebner spent his life in sports. "After Little League," Ebner recounted, "my Babe Ruth team made it to state championship tournament, and my American Legion team went to regionals and nationals." Ebner starred in college baseball at Columbia University, being named captain in his senior year. "Back then, the Ivy League was very strong athletically. It was called the Eastern League, as it included teams from Army and Navy. I played against future major leaguers like Chuck Seelbach, who pitched at Dartmouth and later for the Detroit Tigers, and Pete Varney, who played catcher for Harvard and for the Chicago White Sox."

Post-graduation, Ebner obtained a master's degree and a doctorate in physical education administration. He taught at Columbia, coached its baseball team for thirteen years, and was its athletic director for decades, helping to rebuild the university's entire athletic complex in northern Manhattan. Two of Ebner's four daughters played softball at Columbia.

After more than three decades at Columbia, Ebner retired. He and his wife Virginia relocated to Rockland County, north of the city, to a neighborhood rural enough to remind him of his childhood one. Ebner became director of the county's Jewish Community Center. To date, his four daughters have given him four granddaughters. "I'm surrounded by girls," Ebner said with delight.

When asked about the significance of the summer of '64, Ebner tends to downplay it. "I've done a lot of other great things since then," he noted. "Many other things that mean so much more in the long run."

Two years after the MILL championship, Eddie Godnig's family moved from Staten Island to West Islip, Long Island, because of his father's work. "It was quite a different experience," Godnig explained, "living in the suburbs right near the beach." The near-sighted Godnig, who had an aptitude for science and math, became an optometrist. He worked for two decades in Kittery, Maine, before moving to Alaska in 2003. Godnig now lives in Palmer, Alaska, and still practices optometry although part-time now. "It's wonderful here. I hike, bike, ski, and fish. After all these years in a small town, I can't imagine living in Staten Island as it is now."

Godnig sometimes brings up the 1964 championship in conversations. "It blows people's minds. As for me, I try not to make too big a deal about it."

When Bill Rogers returned to work at Procter & Gamble after leading MILL to the championship, he was honored at a luncheon where he received a standing ovation. The following year, Rogers left his factory job to open up a sporting goods store, Bill's World of Sports, which he owned for fifteen years, followed by a sports pub. Rogers ultimately would coach fourteen All-Star teams and remain affiliated with the Staten Island Little League for more than forty years, wearing various titles including MILL president and District administrator in charge of all the Staten Island leagues. Among his accomplishments was creating a new field complex for MILL on land purchased from the city.

Now in his 80s and living with his second wife, Doreen, in Lakewood, New Jersey, Rogers remains a mentor to Little League players, regularly attending games and giving pep talks and advice. In 2018, when MILL again reached Williamsport, Rogers threw out the first pitch before their first game. "Baseball has been my life," Rogers emphasized, "My love for it has never left me. And never will."

We as a society have learned that demanding success of young athletes must be done with great care and sensitive calibration of competing interests. Bill Rogers' greatest achievement was not coaching a Little League championship team. Rather, it was the foundation he helped create in his own unique manner, along with the significant contributions of parents, relatives, teachers, and others, for the life enjoyed by each of his players.

*

Most of the MILL team members stayed in touch over the decades, facilitated in recent years by social media. Some attended the Little League World Series together to celebrate the 10th- and 25th-year anniversaries of their championship.

In 1999, the entire team was inducted into the Staten Island Sports Hall of Fame. Flying in for that ceremony, it was the first time Godnig had seen his teammates in decades. "It was emotional. I didn't realize how strong our collective bond was. Much changed in all of us, one being that I was of average height back in 1964, but in adulthood I grew to only five feet, six inches, so most of the guys were a lot taller than me. Nonetheless, certain things stay the same. The personality. The demeanor. And the eyes. When you focus on the eyes like I do as an optometrist, people are ageless."

What struck Jay Price, a member of the SISHOF Induction Committee, during that ceremony was the obvious reverence the players, then in their late forties, maintained for Rogers. "When Bill spoke, the players turned their heads and listened as if hearing the voice of God. As if they were kids again."

In late August 2014, nine of the team members gathered in Williamsport for a 50th-anniversary reunion. "When Coach Rogers saw me," Nugent recalled, "he almost had a heart attack because I looked just like my father, who had passed away."

Before the championship game, the MILL alumni were invited onto the Lamade Stadium field. "We stood," Paul recollected, "and waited for the ceremony to begin. On an instinct, I stepped out of formation and walked back to second base. I crouched down, reflecting on it all. Then I hustled back, not wanting to get yelled at."

Days after that World Series ended, the former MILL players rode the Staten Island Ferry to lower Manhattan and retraced their steps up the Canyon of Heroes as guests of the Manhattan Downtown Alliance. At a spot on Broadway below Fulton Street, a granite plaque was installed commemorating their ticker tape parade. Yaccarino encapsulated that special day: "In 1964, we started out at the bottom of Broadway as twelve-year-old boys. By the time we reached City Hall, we were young men."

Dan Yaccarino being introduced to the Little League World Series crowd during the 50th-anniversary commemoration at Williamsport

Jeff Paul being introduced to the crowd

*Bob Nugent, Jeff Paul, and Rich Smiechowski
signing baseballs at Williamsport*

*During the ceremony on Broadway–from left: Don
Quattrochi, Bill Rogers, Rich Smiechowski, Dan
Yaccarino, Greg Klee, Jeff Paul, John Currado*

APPENDIX
"Baseball Heaven on Earth"
by Ed Godnig (August 2014)

The Mid-Island All-Star boys,
In the sensational summer of '64,
Were all so damn cool,
Yet played baseball so damn hot.

They dominated the diamond,
From first to third and right to left,
And all positions in-between,
Boy wonders playing like the Yankees.

Won ten games in a row,
Ended up in Williamsport, PA,
Playing tough for Coach Rogers,
Believing indeed that dreams do come through.

Beat Germany and then the boys of Japan,
Found themselves playing Monterrey, Mexico,
For the Little League World Championship,
Wow, Yac's no-hitter led us to the promised land.

When the Forgotten Borough Reigned

Jump half a century later,
To the uproarious world of 2014,
The boys of '64 are now seasoned men,
With fond memories of reaching baseball heaven.

Yes, heaven on earth, yeah heaven on earth,
Holey moley, we reached heaven on earth,
Yes, heaven on earth, yeah heaven on earth,
Holey moley, we reached heaven on earth.

ACKNOWLEDGMENTS

WRITING THIS BOOK during the 2020–21 pandemic, it served as a wonderful distraction from the incessant gloomy news. As I researched, interviewed, and composed, I was transported back to a non-virtual, Zoom-less time that appeared so much simpler, happier, and innocent. One I could relate to as, in the summer of 1964, I was a nine-year-old baseball-loving boy living happily in Elmhurst, Queens, a few miles from Shea Stadium and the World's Fair, where my dad worked part-time. The MILL championship was an experience I envied, as I never played in an organized sports league of any type.

An example of my living in two time periods came in early December 2020, when I read that Phil Linz, the former Yankee infielder, had died. It instantly brought back memories of chatting with school friends about the famous Linz-Yogi Berra "Harmonica Incident" of August 1964, which kickstarted the Yankees' pennant-winning drive.

You might say that this book owes its existence to an online dating app, which is how my son Craig met his future wife, Emily, the daughter of Jeff Paul. After I learned of

Jeff's summer of '64 experience, the idea of writing this book soon enchanted me.

The introductions to former teammates and the consistent, enthusiastic support provided me by Jeff and Betty were critical. Among other things, I benefited from Jeff being a packrat and keeping an enormous amount of newspaper clippings and other original documents from 1964 that had been gathered by his mom.

I was fortunate to be able to speak with each of the members of the starting lineup as well as with Bill Rogers. Each of them graciously gave his time to my efforts. I thank them for allowing me along for the ride more a half century later.

Also of great help were Joe Nugent, Bobby's older brother, a former MILL All-Star, college baseball player, and longtime sports columnist and broadcaster who is a great expert on Staten Island sports, Gary Schiavone, Bill Roger's son and "technical advisor," and Eddie Sosa, Mike Sosa's youngest son.

I benefited enormously from the work of two team members who are authors in their own right. Ed, also an amateur songwriter, penned *Journey to Williamsport: Memories of a Little League World Champion*, a memoir of that magical summer. And John wrote the yet unpublished *The Joy of Playing and Coaching Youth Baseball,* a comprehensive guide for Little League managers in which he intersperses stories of the 1964 team.

In April 2021, I traveled to Williamsport—my first visit there—and stood at the spot along Route 15 where the MILL players gathered as boys to gaze at their field of dreams. The sight thrilled me also, although nowhere near as much as it did those fourteen kids.

Another part of my research involved viewing the tape of the championship game against Monterrey. As I sat in front of my TV, I imagined what it would be like to be one of the MILL players watching this as a senior citizen, perhaps with his grandkids at his side. My guess is that a good summary of the feelings engendered is the opening of Terence Mann's famous soliloquy: "They'll watch the game, and it'll be as if they dipped themselves in magic waters. The memories will be so thick they'll have to brush them away from their faces."

The ten team members who I interviewed share an everlasting and enviable bond. In addition to them, there were six others who journeyed to Williamsport that summer as part of the MILL All-Star team. Three have passed on: Assistant Coach Bob Klee, Frank Higgins, and John Porcell. I was not able to track down the others. One is Gary Kresge, who started several of the early tournament games in left field. The other two are Mike Troiano and Mickey Wicinski, who were reserves on the team.

Many thanks to Pat Salmon, Staten Island historian extraordinaire, for her insights into life on the Island during the 1960s and the enormous impact of the opening of the Verrazzano-Narrows Bridge. I also greatly appreciate the stories and feedback provided by Jay Price, longtime sportswriter for the *Staten Island Advance* and author of *Thanksgiving 1959*, a wonderful book on old-time Staten

Island high school football. And I'm grateful to Kay "Tubby" Johnston for sharing with me her recollections of becoming the first girl to play in Little League.

A writer needs readers. Much appreciation to my son-in-law, Adam Morris, cousin Steve Lewitzky, and longtime friends Jeff Eimer, Marc Golin, Tom Quaranta, and Saul Zuchman for their valuable comments on a draft of the book.

As with every book I've written, deep thanks to my wife, Linda, for her encouragement, our numerous brainstorming sessions, and her sensitive and thoughtful editing. Distinctly indifferent to baseball, Linda bravely plowed through all the jargon and historical references with good humor. And gratitude to and pride for my talented daughter Arielle Morris, who designed the cover.

This world needs, more than ever, the joy provided to those who play or watch baseball, especially the amateur type such as Little League. May it live on eternally.

I hope you enjoyed this book.
Would you please do me a favor?

Like all authors, I rely on online reviews to encourage future sales. Your opinion is invaluable. Would you please take a few moments now to share your assessment of my book on Amazon or any other book-review website you prefer? Your review will help the book marketplace become more transparent and useful to all.

Thank you very much!

BIBLIOGRAPHY

Alina Durkovic, *From Beach Resort to Bedroom Community: Staten Island and the Impact of the Verrazzano-Narrows Bridge* (Pace University Thesis, 2012)

Angie Mangino, *Meet the People, Experience the Events: 17th Century Tottenville History Comes Alive* (2018)

Bill Cotter & Bill Young, *Images of America: The 1964–1965 New York World's Fair* (Arcadia Publishing, 2004)

Carl Stotz (as told to Kenneth Ross), *A Promise Kept: The Story of the Founding of Little League Baseball* (Zebrowski Historical Services, 1992)

Charles Euchner, *Little League, Big Dreams: The Hope, the Hype, and the Glory of the Greatest World Series Ever Played* (Sourcebooks, 2006)

Danny Brigandi, *Images of Modern America: Williamsport* (Arcadia Publishing, 2015)

David Halberstam, *October 1964* (Ballantine Books, 1995)

Discovering Staten Island: A 350th Anniversary Commemorative History (History Press, 2011)

Doug Elbert, *Look Up, Williamsport!: A Walking Tour of Williamsport, Pennsylvania* (Cruden Bay Books, 2009)

Drew Coolidge, *Coaching Youth Baseball: Coach Like a Champion* (2014)

Edward Godnig, *Journey to Williamsport: Memories of a Little League World Championship* (Northbooks, 2006)

Gay Talese, *The Bridge: The Building of the Verrazzano-Narrows Bridge* (Bloomsbury, 2014)

Gary Gray, *A Levittown Legacy: 1960 Little League World Series Champions* (Mt. Nittany Press, 2019)

Jacob Kornhauser, *100 Moments That Shaped Baseball History* (2018)

James Verdi, *Loyalty and Rebellion* (Documentary, 2019)

Jay Price, *Thanksgiving 1959: When One Corner of New York City Was Still Part of Small-Town America, and High School Football Was the Last Thing Guys Did for Love* (Mountain Lion, 2009)

Jim Bain, *Coaching Youth Baseball* (2018)

Jim Brosnan, *Little League to Big League* (Random House, 1968)

John Currado, *The Joy of Playing and Coaching Youth Baseball* (unpublished)

Johnny Reizer, *Once in a Lifetime: The Story of a National Championship Little League Team* (2019)

Lance & Robin Van Auken, *Play Ball! The Story of Little League Baseball* (Omnibus, 2018)

Lawrence Samuel, *New York City 1964: A Cultural History* (McFarland & Co., 2014)

Little League Official Program (1964 World Series)

Little League Regional Tournament (Burnham Park, Morristown, New Jersey): August 20–22, 1964 (brochure)

Mark Kreidler, *Six Good Innings: How One Small Town Became a Little League Giant* (Harper Collins, 2009)

Moonbeams: Manufacturing Edition (a monthly magazine for employees of Procter & Gamble, September 1964)

Noel Hynd, *The Final Game at Ebbets Field*, (Red Cat Tales, 2019)

Noel Hynd, *The Giants of the Polo Grounds: The Glorious Times of New York's Baseball Giants* (Red Cat Tales, 2018)

Robin Van Auken, *Little League Baseball World Series*, (Arcadia Publishing, 2002)

Souvenir Program: New York State Tournament–August 13–15 (Eastchester Little League, Eastchester, New York)

Steven Wisensale, *How Baseball Has Strengthened the Relationship Between the United States and Japan* (*Smithsonian Magazine*, March 29, 2018)

This Is Little League: Twenty-Fifth Anniversary 1939–1964: A Quarter Century of Service to Youth (1964)

W. William Winokur, *The Perfect Game: An Incredible True Story* (Inspyre Media Press, 2008)

Zachary Brown, *Baseball and the Civil War: Forging America's National Pastime* (*U.S. History Scene* article)

ENDNOTES

[1] Over the next few decades, the Dutch engaged in numerous bloody battles with local Lenni-Lenape tribesmen threatened by the Europeans' encroachment. In 1661, a resolution was negotiated sufficient to allow the Dutch to establish a lasting colony called "Oude Dorp" ("Old Town") on the eastern shore. But only three years later, the English seized control of the Island. In 1667, at the end of the Second Anglo-Dutch War, although the Dutch Republic was victorious, it ceded its colony of "New Netherland," which included Staten Island, to England. The Dutch chose instead to keep what they believed were more valuable possessions, such as the sugar plantations of Suriname. The English renamed the Island "Richmond," in honor of Charles Lennox, the first Duke of Richmond, son of King Charles II by his French-born mistress.

[2] In the summer of 1776, General William Howe and his nine thousand British troops, the largest expeditionary force of the 18th century, evacuated Boston—forced out by General George Washington's brilliant military maneuvers. After landing in Tompkinsville on the northeast end of Staten Island, Howe used the Island as a staging ground for attacking Manhattan and Brooklyn.

On September 11, 1776, days after the British capture of Long Island and less than three months after the Colonies' Declaration of Independence, John Adams, Benjamin Franklin, and Edward Rutledge, representatives of the Second Continental Congress, met secretly with British Admiral Lord Richard Howe to attempt to negotiate an end to the nascent Revolutionary War. The "Staten Island Peace

Conference" was held at the Billop Manor, the residence of loyalist Colonel Christopher Billop, in Tottenville on the southern end of the Island. Admiral Howe, offering clemency, sought to end the war by driving a wedge between the provisional government and General George Washington, but the Americans insisted on recognition of their independence. After three hours, the delegates retired, and the British resumed their military campaign.

The following summer, a failed raid by the Continental Army against British troops became known as the "Battle of Staten Island."

[3] The first tennis court in the U.S. was set up by Mary Ewing Outerbridge, a member of a prominent family who, after playing the game in Bermuda, set up a court at the Staten Island Cricket and Baseball Club.

[4] A well-known one was the "69th Street Ferry," which in ten minutes transported passengers (and their cars) from Bay Ridge across the Narrows to St. George in Staten Island, crossing the path of freighters and ocean liners headed for Manhattan or the open seas.

[5] The Staten Island Ferry originated in 1817, when the Richmond Turnpike Company established a steamboat service from Manhattan to Staten Island. Seven years earlier, Cornelius Vanderbilt, born and raised in Stapleton, had begun his own ferry service from Staten Island to Manhattan when he was only sixteen. That started him down the path toward becoming one of the richest persons in world history.

[6] The abandoned portals, only 150 feet each, remain. They were nicknamed "Hylan's Holes" after then-Mayor John F. Hylan, who championed the failed project.

[7] Moses was able to achieve rapid funding and construction of his projects through his skillful use of the public authority, an autonomous organization that built public works with money raised by issuing bonds, the revenues of which Moses could control and use free from government interference.

[8] That house belonged to Warren Fenley, who played briefly for the Boston Celtics in the early days of the NBA and would become Joe Nugent's high school basketball coach.

[9] The men who worked on the bridge referred to themselves as "iron workers" even though they largely worked with steel.

[10] In October 1964, King, only 35, was awarded the Nobel Peace Prize for nonviolent civil-rights activism. He donated the prize money, valued at $54,600, to the civil rights movement.

[11] "Freedom Summer" was a voter registration drive aimed at increasing the number of black voters in Mississippi. Over 700 mostly white volunteers traveled to Mississippi to join African Americans in fighting against voter intimidation and discrimination at the polls. Three of those volunteers were murdered by a Ku Klux Klan lynch mob protected by local police.

[12] Encouraged by Freidan and other prominent figures, including Gloria Steinem and Bella Abzug, women across America expressed dissatisfaction with their domestic roles. Friedan soon co-founded and become the initial president of the National Organization for Women.

In July 1964, a significant gender barrier was broken when Margaret Chase Smith, Republican Senator from Maine, became the first woman to be nominated for the presidency at a major party convention.

[13] In the early 1960s, Mayor Wagner, concerned about image as the 1964 World's Fair approached, led a campaign to rid New York City of gay bars. The city revoked the liquor licenses of the bars, and undercover police officers worked to entrap homosexual men.

[14] Evidence of this came in July of that year when President Johnson signed a law granting the Little League a Congressional Charter of Federal Incorporation.

[15] Before Carl Stotz formed the Little League, teenage boys could join the American Legion baseball program, formed in the 1920s and still existing today. In 1951, the Babe Ruth League was organized for boys between the ages of thirteen and fifteen years. That same year, PONY Baseball was started, which accepts children and young adults from ages four to 23 and, thus, is competitive with Little League.

[16] Tee Ball (ages 4–7) is educational and involves hitting the ball off a tee. In Farm League (ages 5–8), the coach pitches. Every child must be played, and each is shifted around to experience different positions. Minor League (ages 8–10) is more competitive baseball, with players pitching and rules set to better resemble regular baseball. The crown jewel of Little League baseball is the Major Division, for the 10–12 age group. It is play in this division that ends in the Little League World Series. All-star teams are selected in each League, and a tournament is played at District, Sectional, State, and Regional levels.

[17] In 1949, U.S. Rubber, under its Keds trademark, marketed the first rubber-cleated athletic shoe—the first of many products created specifically with Little Leaguers in mind.

[18] Howard Cosell provided the commentary for ABC Radio.

[19] The main character was "Little" Lulu Moppet. Her best friend was Thomas "Tubby" Tompkins, leaders of a boys' club known as "The Fellers."

[20] Relief wasn't available to Maria Pepe under Title IX , enacted only a few weeks after Maria left her Little League team, because it prohibits gender discrimination in "any education program or activity receiving Federal financial assistance" in elementary or secondary schools or higher education, but without specifying athletics or defining its operative terms.

[21] In 1984, Victoria Roche, an American who played for Brussels, Belgium, became the first girl to participate in a Little League

World Series. In 2014, Mo'ne Davis, playing for the Taney Dragons of Philadelphia, became the first girl to pitch a shutout and win a Little League World Series game. Davis also became the first Little Leaguer featured on the cover of *Sports Illustrated.*

²² Subsequently, Little League organizations in eight Southern states seceded and created a segregated "Dixie Youth" League.

²³ Progress in the integration of Little League baseball occurred during the summer of 1955, when on August 9, the all-black Pensacola Jaycees took on the all-white Orlando Kiwanis, marking the first time an all-black squad played an all-white team in the South.

²⁴ The field was named for the son of the founder of a local newspaper, *Grit,* who served on the board of directors for Little League baseball in the 1950s. A donation from Grit Publishing was used to purchase land where the field is located. Its size was set at approximately two-thirds of a professional baseball field, with the mound moved back from 44 to 46 feet from home plate and fences set at 200 feet (extended to 225 feet in 2006 to allow for more doubles and triples). In 1968, the wood and steel stands were razed, and a concrete stadium was constructed.

²⁵ In 1961, a Senior Division was inaugurated for boys from thirteen to fifteen years old. Within three years, that program grew to a thousand leagues.

²⁶ Jim Barbieri of Schenectady, New York, and Boog Powell of Lakeland, Florida, were the first players to appear in both the Little League World Series (1954—won by Schenectady) and an MLB World Series (1966—won by Powell's Orioles over Barbieri's Dodgers).

²⁷ On February 4, 1964, another Little League alumnus—Terry McDermott—achieved fame by winning gold in the men's 500-meter speed skating race. McDermott was the sole American gold medalist during those Olympics and became a national hero. Five days later, McDermott and his wife Virginia were invited to attend the Ed Sullivan

show in person. That night, for the first time, the Beatles performed on American television, and the McDermotts met them backstage.

[28] Cusack's helpers were John Molino, Jaggs Seaman, Joe Darcy Sr., Joe Darcy Jr., and Jim Darcy.

[29] T-Ball and Farm leagues usually do not schedule tryouts since these divisions are purely instructional and not competitive.

[30] Cattails, also known as "punks," are flowering plants with long, flat, tapering leaves that grow in wetlands.

[31] Procter & Gamble operated a factory at the site from 1907 until 1991, when the soap-making operation was moved to Mexico.

[32] That year, MILL lost to a Waterville, New York, team in the championship game for the New York State title.

[33] Wyso would go on to play baseball at Hartwick College in Oneonta, New York, and coach baseball in youth leagues, Dutchess Community College in Poughkeepsie, and Our Lady of Lourdes High School in Poughkeepsie (which he helped to win a New York State Championship in 2006). Wyso later was a pitching coach for the Bluefield Orioles of the Appalachian Rookie League, an affiliate of the Baltimore Orioles organization. He died in 2018 in a car accident.

[34] An "aspirin tablet" is slang for a fastball that's especially hard to hit due to its velocity and movement—in reference to the difficulty of making contact with something as small as an aspirin tablet.

[35] For many decades, breweries were an important part of Staten Island's economy, providing a good income for thousands of Islanders. In 1964, the Piels Company operated one on the Island in addition to its main one in East New York. In the 1970s, Piels closed the plant and the brand entirely, although the brand was revived in 2018.

³⁶ Most catchers of Cummings' era stood 20 to 25 feet behind the batter, which made it impossible to field a curveball. Cummings' catchers were required to move to standing directly behind the batter. Thus, the introduction of the curveball also radically changed the way catchers fielded their position.

³⁷ One of the early nicknames of the curveball was "Uncle Charlie," derived from the name of Harvard President Charles Elliot, who was opposed to the adoption of the curveball because he considered it to be cheating.

³⁸ In 1964, in spite of injuries, Koufax went 19-5 and notched his third no-hitter in three years.

³⁹ While Rogers wanted his pitchers to throw the 12-6 curveball, he understood that the extensive combination of mechanics necessary made it a difficult pitch to master. The hurler must use a four-seam grip in which the middle finger is placed in the gap between the two seams on the right side and the index finger is positioned directly next to it. The pitcher's thumb is placed on the bottom of the baseball. This grip allows the pitcher to create a high amount of topspin while maintaining control. The pitch is thrown with an exaggerated motion with both the middle finger and the thumb simultaneously moving the baseball toward home plate.

⁴⁰ In 1969, Hurley signed with the Minnesota Twins in the supplemental draft. Unfortunately, his career soon was ended by a torn rotator cuff.

⁴¹ Another example was Ray Culp, a 1953 Little Leaguer who made it to the majors and pitched for a decade with the Phillies, Cubs, and Red Sox. His father taught him the finer points of pitching in their backyard, helping him through Little League, junior baseball, and high school. Culp was forbidden to throw a curveball until his junior year of high school.

[42] One of the National Division team members was Rico Bellini, who went on to play shortstop at Seton Hall University. As captain of the baseball team, he led it to back-to-back College World Series appearances in 1974 and '75. Following his graduation in 1975, Bellini played four seasons of professional baseball in the Cleveland Indians farm system. Bellini and Jeff Paul would play baseball against each other at the Little League, high school, college, and Twyford-Muche sandlot levels. In Joe Nugent's opinion, Paul was the better player and it was unfortunate that he didn't receive the opportunity to compete in the minors and attempt to reach the majors.

[43] The "Baltimore chop" was so named because it was a favorite weapon of the 1890s Baltimore Orioles, who supposedly instructed their groundskeeper to treat the area in front of home plate to make it especially hard.

[44] On Sunday, August 2, the "Gulf of Tonkin incident" took place when the destroyer USS *Maddox* engaged three North Vietnamese Navy warships while on patrol. Two of the North Vietnamese boats fired torpedoes, which the *Maddox* evaded before it and the third boat exchanged gunfire. Two days later, a "second Gulf of Tonkin incident" was triggered by the belief of the commanders of two U.S. Navy destroyers that they had been attacked by North Vietnamese gunboats. President Lyndon Johnson authorized a retaliatory air strike from the carrier USS *Ticonderoga* and delivered a late-night televised address calling on Congress to act. Three days later, Congress overwhelmingly approved a resolution authorizing broad use of war powers to combat North Vietnamese and local Communist attacks.

[45] In 2018, in response to criticism of allowing harm to the integrity of the game caused by use of aluminum bats, Little League adopted the "USA Bat Standard," allowing only aluminum bats designed to perform much like wood ones.

[46] It was not until 2012 that the first team from Africa—the Lugazi (Uganda) Little League—made it to Williamsport.

47 In 2001, the number of regions was doubled to sixteen—eight U.S. teams and eight international teams competing round-robin within their own pool, with the top two teams in each pool advancing to single-elimination play. This ensured that a U.S. team always would compete in the final. That same year, Volunteer Stadium opened to accommodate the tournament's growth. (Lamade and Volunteer Stadiums sit back-to-back and are separated by a concourse.)

In 2011, pools were eliminated, with the eight U.S. teams competing in one bracket and the eight international teams in another bracket. The tournament now is double-elimination until the U.S. championship and international championship games, which remain single-elimination, with those winners advancing to the World Championship game.

48 Pryor was famous for banking in the game-winning shot in Oklahoma University's 1947 NCAA basketball semifinal victory over Texas. OU lost 58-47 to Holy Cross in the championship game.

49 Zamboanga City was stripped of the title, which was awarded to the team they beat in the final, Long Beach, California.

50 The Bronx team was forced to forfeit every game in the tournament they participated in.

51 Ricky Collier, Mobile's starting pitcher, blasted a home run in the fifth that tied the score at 2–2 and singled home the go-ahead run in the sixth inning. Joel Harp, who took over the pitching from Collier in the third inning with one out, a runner on third, and two runs in, pitched scoreless, no-hit ball the rest of the way and contributed a three-run homer in the 6–2 win.

52 After a 24-year hiatus, baseball reappeared as part of the 1936 Olympic Games in Berlin. Although other countries had planned to send teams for the tournament, none of them did, so the U.S. squad split into two teams and played a night game on August 12, 1936 in front of 90,000 spectators in Berlin's Olympic Stadium. The two teams

were named the "World Champions" and the "U. S. Olympics." The World Champions won, 6–5.

[53] McAuliffe was best known for his exploits in December 1944 during the Battle of the Bulge, when he was acting commander of the 101st Airborne Division. At Bastogne, Belgium, the 101st was besieged and encircled by a far larger German force. McAuliffe was delivered an ultimatum to surrender or be annihilated. McAuliffe's response to the German commander was one word—"NUTS!" The 101st held off the Germans until the 4th Armored Division arrived days later to provide reinforcement.

[54] One of the stars of those Olympic games was swimmer Don Schollander, who won four gold medals and set three world records. Schollander was a former Little Leaguer who said, "I learned one thing in Little League. Get the details down pat and the results will speak for themselves."

[55] Speaking of Ty Cobb, MacArthur said, "This great athlete seems to have understood from early in his professional career that in the competition of baseball, just as in war, defensive strategy never has produced ultimate victory."

[56] Of note is that, if MILL hadn't won, it would have been the first and only time the U.S. was shut out of the championship game.

[57] The Monterrey team launched its Little League World Series adventure by crossing the border on foot and walking ten miles to McAllen, Texas, where the first tournament was scheduled. They swept through the Texas and Southern regional tournaments. Along the way, their visas expired, and only intervention by the U.S. ambassador to Mexico permitted them to stay. When the boys arrived via bus in Williamsport, a place they had never heard of until entering the U.S., they carried their clothes in paper bags.

⁵⁸ The end of the game was dramatic. Behind three balls to no strikes on his last batter, Angel came back with two fastball strikes. With the crowd screaming "El Flaco!" Macias ventured a curveball that the batter swung at and missed. The fans exploded. Back home, residents danced in the street upon hearing the radio broadcaster scream, "Campeones del mundo!" President Eisenhower invited the team to the White House, and Hollywood chronicled its miraculous season in a heartstring-tugging movie entitled *The Perfect Game*, starring Cheech Marin.

Led again by César Faz, a onetime batboy and clubhouse attendant for the San Antonio Missions minor league team, Monterrey would return the following year and defeat Jaycee of Kankakee, Illinois, for consecutive titles, the first time that had been accomplished. The staff ace on the 1958 Monterrey team was Hector Torres, who held the Kankakee team to two hits in the championship game. Torres would go on to play for several major league baseball teams after switching his position to shortstop.

⁵⁹ During World War II, Fox, a Jew born and raised in Brooklyn, became a German POW. His Master Sergeant Roddie Edmonds saved Fox's life by declaring, "We're all Jews!" when Nazi officers demanded that Jewish POWs be pointed out.

⁶⁰ The Little League World Series became the longest-running event on *Wide World of Sports*.

⁶¹ After the 1953 season, Veeck sold his stake in the Browns to a consortium that moved the team to Baltimore, where they were renamed as the Orioles. In 1959, Veeck headed a group that purchased a controlling interest in the Chicago White Sox. Following Veeck's acquisition of the team, the White Sox went on to win their first pennant in 40 years. Veeck's innovations included the first "exploding scoreboard" in the major leagues—producing electrical and sound effects, and shooting fireworks whenever the White Sox homered—and adding surnames on the back of uniforms, now a tradition. In 1961, due to poor health,

Veeck sold his share of the White Sox and worked intermittently as a television commentator. He passed away in 1986.

[62] Thomson maintained his entire life that although he knew which pitches were coming during his first three at-bats, he chose not to know what Ralph Branca was going to throw when he came to the plate the final time. Branca never believed that, explaining, "I don't think Bobby understood the ramifications of what stealing signs did. They stole the pennant from the Dodger fans, still the greatest fans who ever lived. They stole the opportunity of Dodger players to go to the World Series and maybe beat the Yankees. They stole the glory and money from the Dodger owners."

During the 2017–18 seasons, members of the Houston Astros used a video camera in the center field seats to film the opposing catcher's signals, which were then relayed to the batter.

[63] The other two were Joe Mormello of Levittown, Pennsylvania, in 1960 and Ted Campbell of San Jose in 1962.

[64] Reaching Williamsport in addition to MILL were South Shore in 1985, 1991, and 2009, the Bronx in 2001, and Harlem in 2002.

[65] It took more than a half century, until 2016, for another team from New York State—Maine-Endwell—to win the World Series.

[66] At the time, Ball was about to premiere the third season of *The Lucy Show* on CBS.

[67] According to Albert Fisher, director of television for the World's Fair: "Somehow, the notorious newspaper columnist Hedda Hopper, who was at one time one of the most powerful columnists in the world, managed to squeeze into the convertible with Lucy. Hopper was known for wearing large outlandish wide-brimmed hats. Her hat not only kept poking Lucy in the eye, more important, Hedda Hopper was upstaging

the star attraction. Lucy became angrier by the minute at Hopper's antics. After a half-hour of this, the beloved TV star turned to me and startled me with a string of four-letter words that would truly make a sailor blush. She made it clear to me that if Hedda Hopper were not out of the car at the next stop, Lucy was prepared to call it quits and leave the Fair!"

[68] Stengel is the only on-field person ever to have worn the uniforms of all four New York franchises. As an outfielder for the New York Giants, he hit the first World Series round-tripper at Yankee Stadium, an inside-the-park shot in 1923. As a manager, he's best known for leading the Yankees during their dynasty years in the 1950s. Upon becoming manager of the hapless Mets in 1962, Stengel quipped, "Can't anybody here play this game?"

[69] Previously the only Asian born man to have played in the majors was Chinese-born Harry Kingman, who enjoyed a "cup of coffee" with the New York Yankees in 1914. Murakami made 54 appearances with the Giants before returning to Japan after the 1965 season. It would take 30 more years until another Japanese-born player, Hideo Nomo, appeared in the majors. Nomo won Rookie of the Years honors in 1995 and went on to have an excellent career, including tossing two no-hitters.

[70] The NY Mets received a ticker-tape parade in 1962 in honor of the return of National League baseball. That year, the Mets would go on to record the most losses (120) of any team in modern major league history.

[71] The restaurant was destroyed in a massive fire in 1977.

[72] With the Silvestri's team also having been inducted into the Staten Island Sports Hall of Fame, Currado holds the distinction of being the only person to go into the SISHOF twice.

[73] A highlight of Nugent's career at Coca Cola came in 1980, when he convinced the largest McDonald's franchisee in Ohio to offer, in order to drive up Coke sales, the Big Mac Combo meal—a burger served with fries and Coke—which became a longtime national and then global trend.

ABOUT THE AUTHOR

JEFF IS THE AUTHOR of fiction and nonfiction books, short stories, and screenplays, for which he has won numerous awards. His first screenplay was the basis for the 2019 film *Crypto,* starring Kurt Russell and Alexis Bledel. A previous book, *Shattered Lives,* was made into a documentary film by MacTavish Productions.

A graduate of Queens College and NYU Law School, Jeff lives with his wife in Cranford, New Jersey.

INDEX

W

Wagner, Roger Jr., 148–152, 160
Walls, Randy, 103–104
Wedemeyer, Albert, 124–125
Weeks, David, 103
Weissglass, Julius, 74
West Highway Little League team, 80–81
West Shore Little League team, 37, 78–79, 171
Westerleigh neighborhood, 32, 34
Wicinski, Mickey, *50*
Wide World of Sports, 123
Wiesbaden, Germany, championship team from, 99, 104–108
Williams, Ted, 117
Williamsport, Pennsylvania
  African-Americans in, 27
  history of, 95–96
  Little League history and, 19–21, 29
  Little League World Series and, 95–97, 99–102
Wilson, Horace, 111
Wonderama, 121
World Series 1964, Yankees-Cardinals, 155–157
World's Fair, New York City, 13, 140–141
Wyso, Peter, 36–39

Y

Yaccarino, Danny, 13, 45, *50*, 51, 53, 59, 63–67, 69, 72, 78–79, 81–82, 86, 88–89, 91–92, 106, 107–108, 119–121, 125, 127, 129–133, 135–136, *138*, 143, 145, 150, 154, 163, 165–168, 175–176, *178*
Yaccarino, Jerry, 128
Yankee Stadium, 154, 155
Yankees, New York, 151
Yastremski, Carl, 67–68

Z

Zamboanga City, Philippines Little League team, 99